Love, Grace, and Happy Gatherings Leigh!

California Cooking and *Southern Style*

100 Great Recipes, Inspired Menus,
and Gorgeous Table Settings

♡ *Frances Schultz* ♡

Frances Schultz

recipes by Stephanie Valentine

Cook w/ heart and soul! — Always!

Skyhorse Publishing

Skyhorse Publishing books may be purchased in bulk at special discounts for sales promotion, corporate gifts, fund-raising, or educational purposes. Special editions can also be created to specifications. For details, contact the Special Sales Department, Skyhorse Publishing, 307 West 36th Street, 11th Floor, New York, NY 10018 or info@skyhorsepublishing.com.

Skyhorse® and Skyhorse Publishing® are registered trademarks of Skyhorse Publishing, Inc.®, a Delaware corporation.

Visit our website at www.skyhorsepublishing.com.

10 9 8 7 6 5 4 3 2 1

Library of Congress Cataloging-in-Publication Data is available on file.

Cover design by Janice Shay and Daniel Brount
Cover photo by Christy Gutzeit
Book design by Janice Shay / Pinafore

Photography by page number:

Deborah Whitlaw Llewellyn 14, 17, 18, 20, 21, 24, 27, 29, 30, 34, 35, 37, 38, 41, 43, 44, 47, 50, 53, 57, 58, 61, 62, 64 (bottom), 67, 68, 70, 72, 75, 76, 79, 80, 84, 89, 93, 94, 95, 96, 97, 99, 100, 101, 103, 104, 106, 109, 111, 114, 116, 121, 122, 124, 130, 133, 134, 137, 138, 142, 146, 149, 162, 165, 168, 169, 175

Aaron Delesie 49, 125, 126, 128, 129, 131, 132, 135, 139, 140, 141, 143, 144, 145

John Fitzpatrick v, 13 (portrait of Stephanie), 152

Mason & Poet 6

Tria Giovan 5, 7, 8, 9, 10, 11, 55 (top), 77, 82, 83

Christy Gutzeit ii, ix, 2, 3, 87, 150, 151, 153, 154, 155, 157

Lauren Porcher 15, 16, 23, 85, 86, 89, 91

Frances Schultz vi, xi, xii, 13, 25, 29, 31, 32, 36, 48, 51, 55 (bottom R-L), 59, 60, 64 (top), 69, 73, 107, 113, 117, 118, 123, 158, 161, 163, 167, 170, 173, 177

Print ISBN: 978-1-5107-4049-5
Ebook ISBN: 978-1-5107-4050-1

Printed in China

California
Cooking
and
Southern
Style

I dedicate this book as both love letter and thank-you note. It is first to my husband Tom and our life here on this beautiful ranch in this beautiful place, the Santa Ynez Valley of California. It is to friend and co-author Chef Stephanie Valentine and her extraordinary skill and creativity. It is to Wyatt and Brie Cromer, to Felipe and Sandra Hernandez, to Patricia Lopez, Juan Garcia, Isaac "Maestro" Bonilla, and Jackie Elliott. To all of you whose hard work, goodness, and grace fills every hill, valley, oak, and vine of this ranch and every page of this book, my deepest thanks.

From left, Maestro, Wyatt, Felipe, Stephanie, and Juan

Contents

A Cottonwood-lined road at Rancho La Zaca after a rain,
oil on panel, by Frances Schultz.

Foreword

By Randall Day and William Hurbaugh

A mainstay of Southern hospitality is inviting the preacher to Sunday supper.

Even if the Southern hospitality is in California.

And even if it's the 21st century and it's the preacher and his husband.

As a gift of unmerited grace, most every one of our Sundays ends, blessedly, at Rancho La Zaca, at table with Frances and Tom. And what tables they have been! Beauty, creativity, conversation, cuisine from the backwoods and around the world (out of this world!). But mostly our Sunday suppers are about friendship and love.

When Frances writes about lifestyle, she writes about more than meets the eye. Substance is served by form, and both create a whole—one isn't more important than the other. Style, cooking, and gathering all combine in expressing exuberant living. As in her recent *The Bee Cottage Story* and now with *California Cooking and Southern Style*, she writes about living in real life. Frances's hospitality *is* her "Southern style."

Martin Buber wrote, "All real living is meeting." Hospitality, as you encounter it here, creates the possibility of coming together and connecting with people face to face and heart to heart—regardless of culture, tradition, race, religion, age, gender, or sexuality.

This book is about things that happen in real time. Technology is not needed (or allowed!) at the table because it distracts us from what is there to feed us. *California Cooking and Southern Style* is about actually experiencing our experiences—embracing the present moment in laughter, delight, awe, confusion, new insights, the unexpected, and all that happens when people meet, person to person.

Frances shows how we can be lured into living, wooed, drawn, even seduced . . . starting with California cuisine and Southern hospitality . . . and leading everywhere.

Hospitality, Heart, and Soul

In a myth of ancient Greece, Baucis and Philemon invite two wandering peasants into their humble village home. In the book of Genesis, Abraham and Sarah welcome three strangers to their tent. Both couples offer the best they can in food, wine, and comfort, with nothing to gain but good will. In turn they receive so much more. Initially unwitting and then believing, these modest hosts had entertained gods and angels. They had glimpsed the divine. Is there not a god or angel in all of us? Isn't that part of what those ancient myths are getting at?

Hospitality is one of mankind's oldest and most sacred rites. It is also a commandment. Loving our neighbor is the heart of hospitality and indeed the heart of life itself: to love. In all my years and articles and books about lifestyle and entertaining and making it all pretty, I have always understood that making people feel welcome was important. What I understand now, though, is that making people feel welcome is *the* importance. The rest is window dressing: food, flowers, linens, lighting, music. Rest assured I *love* the window dressing! It's what I do! It's fun! I'm guessing you do too, or you wouldn't be holding this book right now. But it's fun because it feeds our souls, and it feeds our souls because it is an expression of love. Entertaining at home—or anywhere—making others feel welcome, is a labor and a gift of love.

That I happen to be Southern may account for my apparent genetic predisposition to fix flowers, set tables, and feed people. For generations my South was—and still is in my neck of the Eastern North Carolina woods—a rural patchwork of farms and small towns, often at some distance from one another. People got lonely, so they invited the neighbors, welcomed the newcomers, and cordially abided the strangers passing through. Even among the less well-off, which was much of the South for many years, there wasn't much to show off, but they could be friendly. Even among the more fortunate, in the lean years there was said to be "too much rattlin' of the silver for the fewness of the food." But they made the effort anyway.

The hospitality of Abraham was not conditional. No telling where those desert strangers were from, who their families were, which clubs they were in (or weren't). True hospitality, at home and in the world, like God's love, is not conditional.

In the South today, you'll still find the waiter who asks where you're from and the cashier who has time for a chat. Such freely offered exchanges are an implicit welcome, a tacit invitation to stay a while. Arguably this is true of many small towns and rural areas, including those of our Santa Ynez Valley in California. No doubt this is part of what has resonated with me so deeply here in my new home.

~~~~~~

The extension of hospitality rather grandly called "entertaining" is, in our house, most often simply a few friends for dinner, though we occasionally splash out in more elaborate schemes. But whatever the trappings, we invariably share a meal and thus partake in an ancient ritual.

From the caves of Botswana to the banks of the Euphrates, souls gathered for feasts. Food was prepared, altars festooned, blessings said, wine poured. And then, invariably, Demosthenes drank too much,

Miriam's hair accidentally caught fire, Beowulf banged on about the Visigoths (again), and a harried servant forgot the potatoes. That was and is all part of it. Human beings need food for nourishment, community for comfort, gossip as entertainment, decorating as self-expression, and . . . forgiveness. Meeting these needs does not require a dinner party, but it is the best (and most fun) way I know.

On a deeper level, though, ritual connects us to spirit. No special equipment, training, or religion is required. A ritual can be as simple as a handshake, as bracing as a morning run, as elaborate as a wedding, as entreating as a prayer. But a ritual, however defined or fleeting, distracts us from the everyday and shifts our experience. It alters our way of being in the world, if only for an instant. A ritual both reminds and allows us to be present in that moment, to connect with ourselves, to one another, and to something beyond ourselves in which we all share. Ritual is our connection to the divine.

In writing this book, I feel called to honor the longing for connection itself. A gathering of friends at table is as simple and profound as that, a sacred space in which we nourish our bodies and feed our souls.

If you are one of those people who loves to entertain, I hope you feel both at home and inspired in these pages. If you are someone who loves the idea of entertaining but does not actually do it, or who loves the idea of entertaining but is terrified by it; take heart. Ours are ideas you can use, tables you can set, and meals you can serve whether you live on a ranch or a third-floor walk-up . . . and I've lived in both and places in between.

At my erstwhile little Bee Cottage in East Hampton, I usually entertained outside in the garden and on the covered porch. But more than once we were

weather-spooked indoors and a scramble (or ten) ensued. Yet somehow those parties ended up being just a little bit more fun. There's a sense of adventure about them, a touch of mayhem, like an inside joke everyone's in on and always remembers. Vodka helps.

Remember, the point is not the food, or the flowers, or the showing off. The point is bringing people together, be it with pizza on paper plates or caviar on porcelain. It does not have to be perfect. I have learned to embrace my inner-poster-child of the not-perfect, and I recommend you do the same, in entertaining and in all things, while I'm at it. A relaxed and confident hostess is the first and paramount order of a successful party.

At the ranch we've entertained six ways from Sunday, from "El Morocco" in the barn, to picnics in the vineyard, to trays by the fire. What you will find, though, is that our tables, flowers, and fabulous recipes can work in any setting and with any budget. Let the creative sparks here light your fire, and you will be off and blazing.

Look anew at your possible settings: kitchen, living room, family room, den, fireplace, dining table, coffee table, card table, TV tray, outdoor grill, garden, lawn, porch, terrace, balcony, trees, woods. Maybe you even have one of those treasured relics called a dining room (we, alas, do not). Trust that your tables are there, in your home and in your imagination, just waiting, like your future guests, to be invited to the party.

Here in California, I am blessed to call home this ranch in one of the most beautiful landscapes in the world. It inspires me every day and offers a banquet of possibilities for entertaining, all of which I am privileged, honored, and delighted to share with you.

Welcome to Rancho La Zaca

By way of introducing Rancho La Zaca, perhaps a teensy bit of California history is in order. Since the sixteenth century the Spanish, among others, had been poking around California, but it wasn't until the eighteenth century that serious settlement began, notably as a series of missions, beginning near present-day San Diego and on north. Along the way, they built a few fort-like presidios and a handful of pueblos, of which Los Angeles and San Jose were the most prominent. Then, as kings and queens do to clinch their claims, they granted great swaths of land to worthy subjects, used mostly for ranching. Later, as settlers and natives do under bossy sovereigns, they got restless and annoyed. So annoyed, in fact, that Mexico whupped the Spanish in 1821 and soon made land grants of their own. They also nationalized those Roman Catholic missions quicker than you could say Ave María—because who knew what mischief they might cook up. Fortunately, the old Santa Ynez and Santa Barbara missions near us stand majestically to this day and remain active churches. Of the initial Mexican land grants, our Rancho La Zaca was one of the earliest, in 1838. Ten years on, it was the Americans doing the whupping in the Mexican-American War, which inevitably resulted in tussles over those land grants. Suffice to say that La Zaca remained intact until the 1970s, when its original 4,458 acres were divided into four smaller lots, of which our ranch and vineyard is one.

As for the meaning of "zaca," there is no straight answer. There was an Aztec warrior prince called HueHue Zaca, who was the brother of Montezuma I. The name Zaca may derive from *zacatl*, the Aztec word meaning "grass." I've also read it was named for an ancient Native American site called *Asaca* discovered beneath the cross of highways 101 and 154 in Santa Ynez. And it may have been the Chumash Indian word for "peace." Errol Flynn had a splendid sailing yacht called *Zaca*, which was the Hollywood word for *#nowevenmoregirlswillsleepwithme*. Whatever. To those of us who have lived at one time or another in a place called *Zaca*, it has simply meant home.

The current house was designed by the preeminent American architect Hugh Newell Jacobsen for the actor James Garner and his wife in the late 1990s. As an aside, Mr. Jacobsen was a favorite of Jacqueline Kennedy Onassis and designed her house in Martha's Vineyard. Funnily enough, the Garners bought Rancho La Zaca from a former brother-in-law of Mrs. Onassis, the actor-director Herbert Ross, who was married to Jackie's sister Lee Radziwill. That was before Mr. Garner built the current house, and sadly I have no images of the ranch before then. I never did meet him, but our vineyard manager Felipe Hernandez was his friend and remained close to him until he died in 2014.

We never know where life will take us, do we? If you followed my last book, *The Bee Cottage Story: How I Made a Muddle of Things and Decorated My Way Back to Happiness*, you may recall that I had done just that and was able to regain some clarity and sense of purpose partly through renovating Bee Cottage. As time-honored metaphor for the self, the house showed me the way to my heart. Through the home that I found myself in, I found the self that I could be at home in.

Then as time passed and fortune smiled, I found love again and followed it to California. My new

home is about as far away as you can get from my old home, and in more ways than one. Rancho La Zaca, in Los Olivos, is some three thousand miles and a world away from Bee Cottage in East Hampton. Bee was a hundred-year-old smallish, English cottage-y thing in a village ninety miles from New York City. Rancho La Zaca is a contemporary seven-thousand-square-foot concrete and glass thing in the Santa Ynez Valley, eight miles from the nearest post office.

Alrighty then. And hey, our ability to experience and embrace the new is how we stay young and keep our creativity flowing, right? Disrupting preconceived notions is the precursor to discovery. What I found was that yes, we could make this boxy, modern space warm and welcoming, and we could extend that warmth and welcome to our guests here. And that is what we have tried to do.

With the help of wonderful local landscape designer Puck Erickson, we reconfigured the exterior entry with subtle elevational alterations,

Rancho La Zaca is all about outdoor living. I love our view of the San Rafael Mountains, and how the vineyards are planted among the oak savannas. In fact, our vineyard is called Oak Savanna. At right, a water feature constructed at the entrance to the house resembles the water troughs seen in local cattle pastures.

new plantings, and a water feature to bring some movement and softness to what was a somewhat foreboding façade.

Inside, local interior designer Mary "Dede" Watkins Wood exerted her considerable talents to honor the house's architecture and scale while remaining sensitive to the (our!) human need for gathering and closeness. In what we call the great room, which includes the dining area as there is no dining "room" *per se*, the result is a blend of old and new, with a few treasured antiques, amply proportioned contemporary upholstered pieces, a jumble of art and objects, a bunch of books, and endless dog hair.

Elsewhere, the kitchen remained as was, but the adjacent breakfast nook was adapted to accommodate a comfy banquette and cheery pillows. The original master bedroom became a sitting room, while a room off my husband's bath and dressing area became our bedroom. The guest rooms were given pretty linens and new beds, which is all there was room for because everything is built in. Nonetheless a fresh imprimatur was made and life was good.

Above left, the dining area in the great room. Table and wing chairs from Dennis & Leen. To the right is the kitchen. Opposite, clockwise from top left, our favorite place to have dinner à deux or just to relax and read. Large butterfly painting by Hunt Slonem; small painting by Baret Boisson. A corner of the sitting room for cards, or projects, or maybe dinner one day? Breakfast room pillow fabric from Raoul; banquette, Perennials. The master bedroom is in quiet tones of taupe and blue. Bed from Nancy Corzine.

These old chestnuts: Salsa, hogging the camera in front, then Dually, then "my" Arnold, the baby of the bunch at age sixteen. Horses are a part of life at Rancho La Zaca, and while I don't have much time to ride, I love to stop by and say hello. Horses have such great energy. Just being around them is grounding.

Cook Notes

Now let me tell you about Chef Stephanie Valentine: Trained impeccably at the Culinary Institute of America in New York and a star protégée of late, famed Chicago restaurateur Charlie Trotter, Stephanie whisked her way up the culinary ladder from one prestigious kitchen to the next, including five years as Mr. Trotter's sous chef, then chef de cuisine, and another five years as executive chef at Roxanne's, San Francisco's beloved raw food restaurant. Eventually Stephanie set aside the grueling business of bigtime restaurants for a slower pace and more civilized hours, coming to cook at Rancho La Zaca in 2004, where she has dazzled ever since. And while she appreciated the many beneficial qualities of raw food-ism, she no longer subscribes. Nothing against raw food-ists, but thank goodness.

"What changed your mind?" I asked her one day.

She said, "Because one day I thought, *man, those lamb chops sure do smell good*."

And yet her food is unfailingly healthy. Maybe that is because as a former competitive bodybuilder and current fitness instructor, she is well aware of the benefits of a plant-based diet and the components of good nutrition. She even has my husband eating salads, which he has only recently begun to admit in public.

What follows is but the tip of the soufflé of what this girl can do, bridled as she is by my directions to keep it simple enough for the average home cook with ingredients accessible enough at the Piggly Wiggly in Tarboro, North Carolina, my hometown. We've pretty much kept to that, and where we deviate, we give you fair warning.

A few bits of housekeeping: The first is olive oil. Where a recipe calls for olive oil, we mean extra-virgin always, because it is the most flavorful. The second is butter. Stephanie and I agree on almost everything, except unsalted butter. I just don't see the point of unsalted anything, including butter. But Stephanie uses it and she is the chef. For purposes of this book, some recipes stipulate "unsalted butter" and others state only "butter." The latter implies you may choose either salted or unsalted. Moreover, you always taste and adjust your seasonings regardless of the recipe, and you know that. But don't be afraid of salt! It's the single most underrated cooking ingredient there is. Salt and pepper means coarse or kosher salt and freshly ground pepper. Oh, and red chili flakes are the same as red pepper flakes. Chili flakes just sounds more California-like.

The *California Cooking* in the title is as much about place as it is about food, but one so often determines the other, doesn't it? Stephanie notes that we all cook and eat differently depending on where we are in the world. The Central Coast region where we live is blessed with a nearly year-round growing season and some of the best farmers and winemakers in the country. We delight in the lettuces and greens and glory in artichokes, avocados, broccoli rabe, fennel, kale, spinach, and herbs of all ilk. We take pride in our artisanal purveyors of dairy products, beef, lamb, pork, and poultry. The catches of our regional fishermen include white seabass, salmon, rockfish, and ridgeback prawns. The nuts California is known for are not only politicians, they are also almonds, pistachios, and walnuts, and are frequent ingredients in our food. Same goes for our gorgeous fruits and herbs. Who knew that olives and mint in a humble green salad would take

it somewhere new? And oh, the flowers!

And the wine! A quick word about the wine: We love it. The vineyards at Rancho La Zaca yield harvests of chardonnay, sangiovese, syrah, and tempranillo, with which our winemaker friends and clients produce sublime vintages. But as wine is such a broad and complex topic so thoroughly and intelligently discussed elsewhere by others way better versed in it than I, I will leave it here. You can't kiss all the boys, my mama used to say.

In cooking we use the freshest ingredients and embrace the wonderfully diverse cultures that have melded into California cuisine—a "howdy" from the Southwest, an "hola" from Mexico, a touch of Asia, a whiff of the Middle East, a salute from the Provençal and Tuscan country sides. Then there's a "hey y'all" from the South, obviously.

We chose and created recipes here for what we love to eat ourselves. Our aim is not to be startlingly original or innovative, and the recipes aren't complicated. Some do take time. It's a labor of love. No one says it's a "nothing-to-it" of love. Besides isn't the creating half the fun? If some recipes appear long, fear not, we're being thorough.

So often the host's challenge is not in finding a good recipe or two, but in figuring what to serve with what. We've solved that with our menus, but feel free to mix and match. Same with the recipes themselves. Try our foolproof versions, and then experiment as you will. Like entertaining and indeed in any art form, the fun is knowing the rules and then knowing how to break them. The important thing is the pleasure, and the point is having fun. That's what's good for the soul, and therefore it's good for everything.

Menu

Heirloom Tomato Salad
with Queso Fresco

Chili Verde

Grilled Zucchini

Tortilla Chips
with Guacamole
and Pico de Gallo

Cornmeal Pound Cake
with Strawberries
and Vanilla Ice Cream

Chapter 1
Welcome to the Valley

How we do love our Santa Ynez Valley. Which, by the way, I did not know before coming to it. My worldly travels had me hither and yon, but somehow I'd missed this gorgeous enclave a stone's throw from Santa Barbara. It was worth the wait. Years ago on a road trip my husband Tom stopped by here and thought it was the prettiest ranch country he had ever seen. He knew then he wanted to have a ranch here one day, and here we are. And we love nothing better than sharing it with family and friends.

On this occasion we hosted a party for the families and out-of-town guests of dear friends marrying off their only daughter. As the groom and many guests were East Coasters like me, we thought an introduction to West Coast ranch and wine country might be a nice way to welcome them on the Thursday before the wedding weekend began.

Good, simple food and plenty of it is our mantra for a meal feeding more than twelve. This super crowd-pleasing menu of melded California-Southwest-Mexican flavors struck just the right chord and could all be prepared in advance and served at room temperature or easily warmed.

Smart-casual-cowboy seemed specific enough, not too taxing, yet offered opportunities for creativity. I'm not huge on costume parties, though I think themes are fun and inspiring for everything from food and décor to attire and music. It adds to the festive air and gets people into the spirit.

One of the things I like about giving parties is what they can teach us about life. Something is going to go awry, probably at the last minute. Roll with it, honey. You've heard of the Santa Ana

Winds? They normally occur between October and March, but they don't always bother to check with the calendar. So rude! They can be full-on even in June, thank you, and just in time for one's outdoor party. Fortunately, they died down after sunset, but we couldn't wait until then to fix the flowers and set the tables. Whatever wasn't tied down took flight. The fabulous flowers by Mindy Rice all tumbled over, candles blew out, napkins soared, hats helicoptered, and skirts sailed (not all bad in the eyes of a nearby cowboy or two). Unflappable Mindy

scrambled for heavier containers, stuffing the flowers in Solo cups (yes, red) and plopping them inside the containers with no one the wiser. Large hurricane lanterns rescued the candles, and by the way, hurricanes are always a good idea for outdoor candlelight. The key is not to panic. Some solution will present itself. And if it doesn't, well, laugh it off and your guests will too—if they notice, which they won't. Giving a party is not heart surgery. Your friends are honored to have been invited and happy to be there. Promise. Particularly in a setting as magical as this one.

Speaking of, most of the flowers and table settings you will see in this book are done by me, but when my schedule forbids it, and if I'm lucky, my go-to is the incomparable Mindy Rice, who stepped in here with her brilliant décor ideas and gorgeous arrangements, and God bless her. Another life lesson: Ask for help when you need it, even with the bits you know how to do and especially with the bits you don't. Have the conversation between your pride and your pocketbook, and eliminate as much fuss and bother as you can.

And no matter what, remember that if you have fun, your guests will too. If you are nervous and uptight, so will they be. Obvious I know, but sometimes the hosts become so wrapped up in the production or the impression they're making that they forget the reason they are having the party in the first place, which is to gather together and have fun.

Heirloom Tomato Salad
with Queso Fresco
Serves 8 to 10

The juice from the tomatoes drips down into the cheese with the lemon and olive oil and makes a wonderful sauce. This is also a nice dish to bring to a summer potluck. It holds up well and leftovers are delicious the next day. Serve it with crusty bread, pita, or tortilla chips. Can also be made with feta cheese.

6 tablespoons olive oil
3 tablespoons lemon juice
2 teaspoons chopped fresh thyme
8 ounces queso fresco or feta cheese
1 small sweet onion, chopped
3 large heirloom tomatoes (about 2 pounds), seeded
   and chopped
Salt and pepper

Make the dressing by whisking together the olive oil, lemon juice, and thyme.

Spread the cheese onto a serving platter, or if serving plated as a first course, divide the cheese between the salad plates. Mound the onions and tomatoes on top of the cheese. Drizzle with the dressing and season with salt and pepper.

This can be made an hour ahead of time and left at room temperature. If you make it earlier in the day, cover and refrigerate, and bring to room temperature before serving.

Opposite: We call this part of the ranch "the old picnic area," but I have no idea why, or if there is a "new" picnic area for that matter. But it is a level clearing surrounded by vineyards and anchored by two enormous oaks that are wrapped in lights. A firepit and partial outdoor kitchen make it a great place for parties. The wines served this evening were from premier Valley winemakers and dear friends Andrew Murray (bottle pictured) and Jim Clendenen of Au Bon Climat. These gorgeous flowers were by Mindy Rice.

Chile Verde

Serves 8 to 10

Serve this with rice or warm corn tortillas. The recipe calls for pork, but it can just as deliciously be made with chicken or with any combination of leftover meat. You may also add any vegetables you like, or omit the meat altogether and replace it with potatoes and butternut squash for a vegetarian version. The leftovers make great nachos!

3 pounds boneless pork shoulder,
   cut into 1-inch cubes
2 teaspoons salt
1 teaspoon ground black pepper
1 tablespoon chili powder
1 large onion, chopped
3 cloves garlic, minced
1 jalapeño pepper, chopped
8 poblano peppers
2 pounds tomatillos, husked and washed
¼ cup + 2 tablespoons vegetable oil
1 cup chicken stock or water
2 bay leaves

For the garnish
Prepare ½–1 cup of each of the following:
   Chopped cilantro
   Chopped onion
   Chopped avocado
   Chopped cabbage
   Lime wedges

In a large bowl, stir together the pork, salt, pepper, chili powder, onion, garlic, and jalapeño, and let sit for 30 minutes.

> **A whole poached chicken will yield about 4 cups of meat, as well as stock to use or save for later.**

Preheat a gas grill to high or preheat the oven broiler. Rub the poblanos and the tomatillos with 2 tablespoons of oil and grill or broil, turning, until the poblano skin is blackened and the tomatillos are cooked and charred in spots, about 6 to 8 minutes. Place the poblanos in a bowl and cover with a cloth or plastic wrap to steam while they cool. Place the tomatillos in a separate bowl and cool to room temperature, then transfer with the juices to a blender and puree. Peel, seed, and slice the poblanos into ¼-inch-thick strips.

Heat a Dutch oven over medium-high heat. Working in batches, add the remaining oil and the pork and brown on all sides. Put all the pork back in the pot and add the tomatillo puree, the poblano strips, jalapeno, stock or water, and bay leaves. Bring to a simmer, cover, and cook over low heat, stirring occasionally, for about 1½ to 2 hours or until the pork is fork tender.

Remove bay leaves and serve with the garnishes on the side.

Note: If you use pre-cooked chicken, you can reduce the overall simmering time to 45 minutes.

Grilled Zucchini

Serves 8 to 10

Zucchini is one of those generous vegetables of which there always seems to be an abundance. This recipe may be used for a variety of vegetables but we especially like it with the delicious zucchini from our seemingly bottomless California farm stands. If you like, add little lunchbox peppers and onions for zest and color.

3 pounds small zucchini, ends trimmed and
   cut in half lengthwise
3 tablespoons olive oil
1 clove garlic, mashed
¾ teaspoon each salt and freshly ground pepper
Squeeze of lemon or dash of sherry vinegar

Preheat grill to medium high or broiler on low setting.

Toss the zucchini, olive oil, garlic, salt, and pepper together in a bowl. If grilling, cook on each side for 3 to 4 minutes, turning halfway through each side to create grill marks and to cook evenly. If oven broiling, cook each side for 2 to 4 minutes, checking and shaking the pan halfway through.

Arrange on a platter and squeeze with lemon or give a sprinkle of sherry vinegar.

Tortilla Chips
with Guacamole and Pico de Gallo

Avocados made their way to California thanks to one Judge R. B. Ord of Santa Barbara, who imported the tree from Mexico in 1871. Thank you, Judge! If you're in the area, Stephanie swears by the 80-year-old avocado trees at Hilltop and Canyon Farms in Carpenteria.

Guacamole
Makes 3 cups

3 large ripe avocadoes
2 tablespoons chopped red onion
½–1 jalapeño, seeded and chopped
4 tablespoons chopped cilantro
Juice from 1–2 limes
Salt

Remove the pits from the avocados and scoop it into a bowl. With a fork, mash the avocado with the red onion, jalapeño, cilantro, lime juice, and salt. Press plastic wrap directly onto the entire guacamole surface and refrigerate until ready to serve.

Pico de Gallo
Makes 2 cups

3 ripe tomatoes, or 6 Roma tomatoes, chopped
½ cup finely chopped red onion
1 jalapeño, seeded and chopped
½ cup chopped cilantro
Juice from 1 lime
Salt

In a bowl stir together the chopped tomato, red onion, jalapeño, cilantro, lime juice, and salt. Adjust the seasoning and refrigerate until serving.

Tortilla Chips
Makes 72 chips. Count on about 1½ to 2 whole tortillas per person.

4 cups vegetable oil, or as needed
12 corn tortillas, cut into 6 wedges each
Sea salt

In a large skillet or deep fryer, heat the oil to 350°F. If using a skillet, you will need enough vegetable oil to maintain a 1-inch depth in the pan.

Working in batches, use a spoon or spatula to carefully lower the tortillas into the hot oil. Stir and turn until golden brown and crisp, about a minute. Remove from the oil, drain on paper towels, and sprinkle with salt to serve.

Cornmeal Pound Cake
with Strawberries and Vanilla Ice Cream
Makes 2 (9-inch) loafs or 1 Bundt cake

This cake is inspired by a similar one served at Coco Pazzo in Chicago. Great on its own or served with ice cream and berries or peaches.

For the Cake

1½ cups cake flour

¾ cup medium grind cornmeal or polenta

1 teaspoon baking powder

¼ teaspoon salt

¾ cup butter, room temperature

½ cup almond paste

1¼ cups sugar, separated

7 large eggs, separated into whites and yolks

1 cup heavy cream

1 teaspoon vanilla extract

½ teaspoon almond extract

For the Glaze

¼ cup butter

1 cup powdered sugar, sifted

¼ cup milk

½ teaspoon vanilla extract

½ teaspoon almond extract

For the Fruit

1 pint strawberries, hulled and quartered; or 2–3 peaches, peeled and sliced

2 tablespoons sugar

1 teaspoon lemon juice

For the Cake: Butter and flour 2 (9-inch) loaf pans or 1 Bundt pan. Preheat the oven to 375°F.

Sift together the flour, cornmeal, baking powder, and salt. Place the butter in a large mixing bowl and beat until light in color, about 5 minutes. Add the almond paste and beat 2 minutes more, until fluffy. Add in 1 cup of the sugar and beat for 5 minutes more, until pale in color. Add the yolks one at a time, beating after each. Add the dry ingredients alternately with the cream in thirds, beginning and ending with the dry ingredients. Stir in the vanilla and almond extracts. Combine the egg whites with ¼ cup of the remaining sugar and whip to form soft, shiny peaks. Fold egg white mixture gently into the batter. Pour mixture evenly into the prepared pans and bake for 1 hour or until a toothpick inserted in the center comes out clean. Remove from the oven and let cool in the pan for 10 minutes then remove to a wire rack. Spread on the glaze while the cake is warm, and cool completely. Serve with the berries and vanilla ice cream.

For the Glaze: Warm the butter and whisk in the sifted powdered sugar, milk, and extracts.

For the Fruit: Mix the strawberries or peaches in a small bowl with the sugar and lemon juice. Let sit at room temperature for at least 30 minutes and up to 2 hours before serving.

I love this picture of His Grace and me. He is the most wonderful host and covers for me beautifully when I am running around like a headless chicken.

Vanilla Ice Cream

Makes 3 cups

You will need an ice cream machine for this recipe. Homemade ice cream doesn't have gums or excess sugars, so it becomes quite hard after several hours in the freezer. Let it soften at room temperature for 5 to 10 minutes before serving.

   Note: Tempering egg yolks prevents them from cooking into scrambled eggs.

1 cup whole milk
½ cup half and half
½ cup heavy cream
½ vanilla bean, split and scraped (optional)
Pinch salt
6 tablespoons sugar, divided
4 egg yolks
1 teaspoon vanilla extract

In a 2-quart saucepan over medium high heat, put the milk, half and half, cream, vanilla bean seeds and pod, and salt. Sprinkle in 3 tablespoons of sugar and, to keep it from scorching, do not stir as you allow the mixture to come to a simmer. While the milk is heating, whisk the egg yolks with the remaining 3 tablespoons of sugar in a large bowl. Stirring constantly, add about half of the hot milk mixture a few tablespoons at a time to temper the yolks (and prevent them cooking into scrambled eggs!). Return the yolk and cream mixture back to pan over medium heat and continue stirring until the mixture is slightly thickened and coats the back of a spoon. Strain into a bowl, stir in the vanilla extract, and chill thoroughly. Freeze according to the manufacturer's directions.

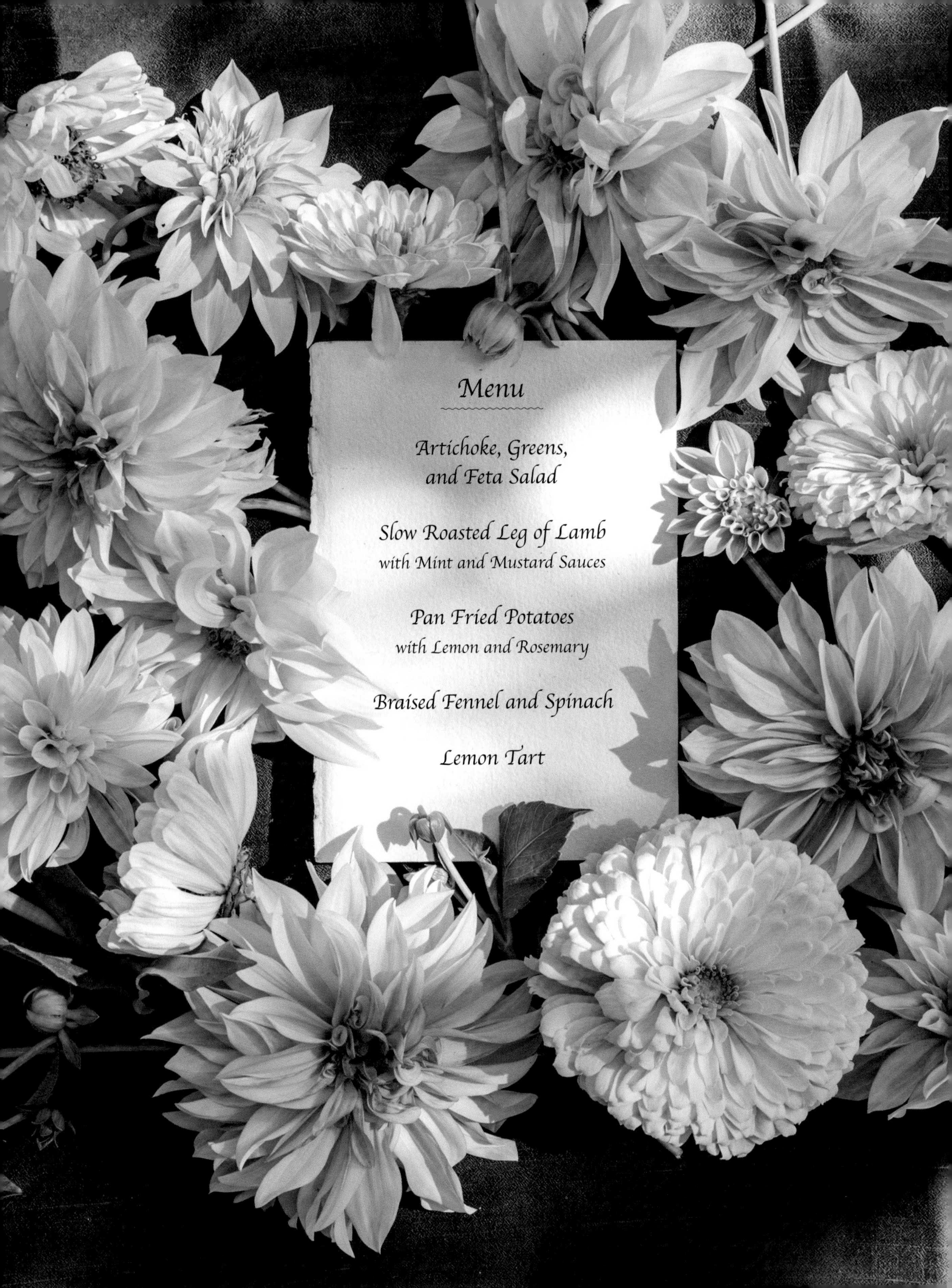

Menu

Artichoke, Greens,
and Feta Salad

Slow Roasted Leg of Lamb
with Mint and Mustard Sauces

Pan Fried Potatoes
with Lemon and Rosemary

Braised Fennel and Spinach

Lemon Tart

Chapter 2
Dinner in the Olives

I should call this chapter "Surprise," not because it was a surprise for the guest but because it was a surprise for the hostess—hello, as in moi. As in your significant other, entirely unbeknownst to you, has agreed to host a dinner for sixty at your house? Are you reading this from jail because you shot him? I get it, but do try not to shoot people verbally or otherwise, regardless of provocation. It's hard to take back. I rallied and we had a ball. Note to self: This is often the case when I can get my knickers un-knotted long enough to find the fun in a thing. Thank you, Mary Poppins.

As Ms. Poppins would say, "Spit spot." The problem was time, and little of it. The solution was our already beautiful arbor of olive trees and the addition of festive lighting. Lighting is an important element in any space, and is especially important to parties for the mood it creates. Café lights are instantly inviting and festive, and candlelight is always pretty, unfailingly romantic, flattering, affordable, and enchanting.

The menu evokes the flavors of the South of France, a part of the world I love and of which the Santa Ynez Valley landscape reminds me daily, our beloved olive trees especially. Artichokes, olives, fennel, spinach, mustard, mint, lemon, and the unmistakable aroma of roasting lamb with garlic and rosemary. What could be better? The sauces for the lamb are super easy to make and delicious. The

mint sauce is more tangy than sweet, which is, like, ten thousand times better than the super-sweet grocery store variety. The fennel and spinach are a lovely combination, and the potatoes are to die for. The lemon tart is perfect. I would totally cheat and use a ready-to-roll-out crust, but that is lazy me. Don't be like me. Make the crust; it is as good as the filling and worth the effort.

Artichoke, Greens, and Feta Salad

Serves 6

Caramelized onions are this recipe's secret weapon. Any combination of greens will work. Here we used baby kale, frisée, and pea shoots (if using frisée, trim and discard the tough outer green leaves and use the curly pale inner leaves.) For the herbs: mint and dill are great, but use what looks good that day. The artichokes and onions can be prepared ahead, refrigerated, and warmed to serve. Baby artichokes may be used here as well, just be aware they will take less time to cook. Meyer lemon juice and preserved Meyer lemon zest are especially good in this salad.

Note: Stephanie would not be caught dead using frozen artichoke hearts, but I would. Just saying.

Onions

1 tablespoon olive oil
1 onion, sliced into rings about ⅛-inch thick
1 tablespoon butter
2 tablespoons lemon juice
Salt and pepper

Artichokes

6 globe artichokes
1 lemon, halved
4 tablespoons olive oil, divided
¼ cup chopped onion
2 tablespoon chopped carrot
2 tablespoons chopped celery
1 clove garlic, smashed
1 teaspoon chopped thyme leaves
Salt and pepper

Salad Greens

4 cups (or 2 bunches) greens, cleaned and trimmed
½ cup mint leaves, torn
½ cup dill sprigs
¼ cup olive oil
2 tablespoons lemon juice
½ cup chopped Kalamata olives
½ cup crumbled feta cheese
Salt and pepper

For the Onions: In a 10-inch sauté pan over high heat, add the oil and the onions, stirring to coat. Reduce the heat to low and add the butter, cooking for 30 to 40 minutes, stirring occasionally, until the onions are evenly golden brown. Stir in the lemon juice, season with salt and pepper, and set aside.

For the Artichokes: While the onions are cooking, prepare the artichokes. Peel the artichokes by first removing the leaves down to the tender pale leaves in the middle. With a serrated knife, cut the pale leaves away just above where they meet the heart and cut the stem from the base of the artichoke. With a paring knife, carefully trim the tough green outer skin on the stem and around the heart. Place the peeled artichokes in a bowl of cold water with juice from half the lemon. Leave the lemon half in the water.

Put a 2-quart sauce pan over high heat and add a tablespoon of olive oil. Sauté the onion, carrot, celery, and garlic for 2 to 3 minutes until starting to soften and brown. Add the peeled artichokes and just enough water to cover. Put a paper towel or small clean dish towel over the top of the artichokes to keep them fully submerged. Bring to a boil, then reduce the heat and simmer for 15 to 20 minutes, until the artichokes are just fork tender. Drain and cool.

Using a spoon, scoop out the furry choke from the center and cut each into 6 wedges.

Heat a 12-inch sauté pan over high heat, add 3 tablespoons of oil, and sear the artichokes for about 6 minutes on all sides. Add the chopped thyme and onion mixture at the very end and season with the juice from the remaining lemon half, salt, and pepper. Remove from the heat and set aside.

To assemble the salad: Divide the artichoke-onion mixture among six plates or on a single platter. Toss together the greens, mint, dill, olive oil, and lemon juice and mound this on top of the artichokes. Sprinkle with the Kalamata olives and crumbled feta. Season to taste with salt and pepper.

Slow Roasted Leg of Lamb
with Mint and Mustard Sauces
Serves 6 to 8

Marinate the lamb at least 3 hours before cooking. If you want to serve a bone-in leg, allow a bit of extra cooking time. This marinade is also good for chicken, fish, and shrimp. If your roast is larger than 3 pounds, roast 20 minutes per pound, or to internal temperature of 135°F for medium-rare.

Lamb Roast

3 pounds boneless leg of lamb
¼ cup olive oil
6 cloves garlic, minced
2 tablespoons smoked paprika
1½ tablespoons salt
1 tablespoon chopped fresh rosemary
1 teaspoon pepper
1 teaspoon sugar
2–4 cups white wine (or combination wine and water)
½ cup Dijon mustard, for the sauce

Tie the leg of lamb with butcher's twine and place in a shallow dish. Stir together the olive oil, garlic, smoked paprika, salt, rosemary, pepper, and sugar, and rub over the lamb (if you have a nice, fatty leg of lamb, trim the fat to ¼-inch and score the fat at 1-inch intervals to allow the rub to penetrate). Refrigerate for 3 hours or longer, and remove from the refrigerator 1 hour before cooking.

Preheat the oven to 425°F.

Place the lamb on a rack in a small roasting pan and place in the bottom third of the oven for 15 minutes. Pour enough wine into the roasting pan to be about ¼-inch deep. Reduce heat to 300°F and roast for 60 to 80 minutes, or until the lamb reaches an internal temperature of 135°F for medium-rare. Add more water or wine as needed to maintain the ¼-inch depth of liquid. Remove the lamb from the oven and from the pan, loosely cover with foil, and allow to rest for at least 30 minutes before slicing.

While the lamb is resting make the mustard sauce: Pour all the juices into a small saucepan, scraping up the bits from the bottom of the pan. You should have about 1 cup. Whisk in the Dijon mustard and warm to serve.

Mint Sauce

Fresh mint sauce has been served with lamb since medieval times. We much prefer this more savory version to the sugary mint jelly found in grocery stores (yuck). If you like a bit of spice, and we do, add a chopped, roasted jalapeño.

2 cups mint leaves
2 tablespoons sugar
½ teaspoon salt
1 jalapeño pepper, roasted, seeded, and chopped (optional)
¼ cup balsamic or red wine vinegar

Chop the mint leaves with the sugar, salt, and chopped pepper (if using) until very fine, place in a bowl, and stir in the vinegar. Adjust the seasoning to taste.

> **Of course you read recipes all the way through before beginning, right? Unless you are me, who has learned the hard way. Do as we say, not as we wish we did.**

Lordy! This platter could be its own float in the Rose Bowl Parade. I got a little carried away. Better to err on the side of simplicity . . . Note to self . . .

Pan Fried Potatoes
with Lemon and Rosemary
Serves 8

Freshly dug potatoes from your local farmers market will make this a very special dish.

3 pounds small Yukon gold or other new potatoes
4 tablespoons olive oil
2 tablespoons butter
1 teaspoon salt
½ teaspoon pepper
1 clove garlic, chopped
1 shallot, chopped
2 sprigs of rosemary, leaves only
Zest and juice from 1 lemon, separated

Place the potatoes in a pot and fill with water so the potatoes are covered by 1 inch, then bring to a boil. Cook 15 to 20 minutes or until the potatoes are just tender all the way through. Drain and cool. This may be done several hours ahead.

Heat the olive oil in a 12-inch cast iron pan or sauté pan. Crush the potatoes slightly by pressing with the heel of your hand and carefully place in the hot oil. Add the butter, salt, and pepper, and cook on one side until golden brown, about 4 to 5 minutes. Turn the potatoes to the other side, and add the garlic, shallot, rosemary, and lemon zest. Cook until golden brown on the second side, a few minutes more. Sprinkle with the lemon juice and season with more salt and pepper as needed.

Lighting
Lighting is so important and so easily made atmospheric. Install rheostars on all overhead fixtures if they're not already. Before a party, switch out high wattage bulbs for low. Put tons of votives everywhere, and presto, instant ambiance and enchanté. Yeah baby.

Braised Fennel and Spinach

Serves 8

This is a great side dish for any meat, and it can be a meal in itself tossed with pasta and Parmesan cheese. See note below.

3 tablespoons olive oil
4 large fennel bulbs, trimmed and cut lengthwise
   into 6ths
1 clove garlic, sliced
1 shallot, sliced
Pinch of red chili flakes
½ cup water or chicken stock
1 teaspoon salt
¼ teaspoon pepper
2 bunches spinach, stemmed and washed

Heat the olive oil over high heat in a 12-inch Dutch oven. Lay in the fennel pieces and sear on both sides, about 2 minutes per side. Add the garlic, shallot, and red chili, stir quickly, and add in the water or stock, salt and pepper. Reduce the heat, cover, and cook until the fennel is tender, about 12 minutes, adding more water or stock as needed to keep ¼-inch of liquid on the bottom of the pan. When the fennel is tender, increase the heat to high and gently stir in the spinach just until wilted. Season with salt and pepper and a drizzle of olive oil.

Variation: For a savory pasta dish, toss the fennel and spinach mixture with fettuccine (or any pasta) and ½ cup or so of Parmesan cheese. Intensify the flavor with an anchovy or two sautéed until dissolved in ¼ to ⅓ cup of olive oil.

Lemon Tart

Serves 10 to 12

This is the perfect lemon tart, perfectly balanced, with a perfect filling-to-crust ratio. The world, alas, is full of under-baked pie crusts. A properly baked pie crust should be nice and brown and cooked all the way through, hence the name pie crust and not pie-soggy-bottom-thing. Follow the directions for the crust to a T, and make the lemon curd while the tart crust is baking. If you do not have a removable-bottom tart pan, a regular pie pan will do.

Note: Whole lemons zapped in the microwave for 30 to 60 seconds will be extra juicy, but caution: Lemons zapped too long in the microwave will be extra messy, because they will explode.

Tart Crust

9-inch round tart pan with removable bottom

3 ounces unsalted butter

1 tablespoon vegetable or olive oil

3 tablespoons water

1 tablespoon sugar

½ teaspoon salt

1¼ cups all-purpose flour

Lemon Curd

Zest of 1 lemon

1 cup freshly squeezed lemon juice (about 4 or 5 lemons)

1 cup sugar

10 tablespoons unsalted butter

4 whole eggs

4 egg yolks

For the Crust: Preheat the oven to 410°F. Combine the butter, oil, water, sugar, and salt in a metal bowl and place in the preheated oven for 15 minutes, until the butter is melted and just starting to brown. Remove from the oven and stir in the flour straight away, being careful with the hot bowl. Stir just until the dough comes together. Reserve a raspberry-size piece of dough for later. Press dough evenly up the sides of the pan and then firmly onto the bottom. Prick crust with a fork and bake for 18 to 22 minutes, or until golden brown. Remove from the oven and fill in any cracks with the reserved dough. Place back in the oven for 4 minutes more.

For the Curd: Preheat the oven to 350°F.

Combine the lemon zest, juice, sugar, butter, whole eggs, and egg yolks into a heavy-bottom, 2-quart saucepan over medium heat. Stir with a wooden spoon until the butter is melted and the curd thickens and starts to bubble, about 5 minutes, and stir and cook 30 seconds more. Remove the pan from the heat. Strain the curd into a bowl using a fine mesh sieve. (Straining is optional, but it does remove the lemon zest and any bits of cooked egg.)

Pour the curd into the tart shell and bake for 6 minutes. Let cool to room temperature, then chill before serving. Serve as is or with whipped cream. This tart holds well and can be made a day ahead.

Menu

Spicy Melon Soup

Deviled Eggs
with Smoked Salmon

Grilled Pimento Cheese Sandwiches

Summer Squash Salad
with Pistachios, Apricots,
and Goat Cheese

Fried Chicken, Extra Crispy

Coleslaw
with Fresh Herbs

Corn-Bacon-Cheese Muffins

Butterscotch Banana Pudding

Chocolate Brownies

Chapter 3
Summer Celebration by the Pond

Warm summer days are perfect for picnics by the pond. One of the many great things about California is that summer days don't stand on ceremony with the seasons, and we have nearly year-round picnic weather here. Picnics and summer just go together, though, and the 4th of July at Rancho La Zaca is a favorite for us.

This raises the issue of the annual such-and-such party, about which there are pros and cons. On the one hand, they are a lovely tradition, a gift to all included, a great anticipation, and a joy. On the other hand, they're not. There are no rules here. Entertaining is at its heart an act of generosity and of love, and far be it from me to discourage either. But when it begins to feel like an obligation, don't do it.

A large, informal gathering outdoors lends itself to a buffet and even better to a glorified picnic. As at a picnic, all the food should taste good at room temperature. Keep the menu simple and the platters abundant. It is better to have lots of a few than a few of lots, the latter of which smacks more of pot-luck than picnic. Nothing wrong with pot-lucks but that's not why you bought this book.

This menu is perfect for a gathering of many or as an informal dinner for a few, and all can be prepared in advance. We've chosen classic picnic favorites and added our own California-Southern spin. I love to pass small servings of soup—hot or cold—as a first course before sitting down, and the chilled spicy melon soup is summery, refreshing, and a bit unexpected.

The world seems to have discovered Southern delicacies like pimento cheese, but when we first started serving it at the ranch ten years ago, people said pi-*what*? I looked at them like they were from Mars, which some Californians are. Southerners know pimento cheese by the time they are embryos. Every now and then a California guest might say, "Oh, I remember my aunt in Virginia used to make that." But still. Even fried chicken was kind of a novelty to my California friends back then, and they

would try to eat it with a knife and fork, which I know technically you are supposed to do unless you are at a picnic, but really?

Stephanie's version of Butterscotch Banana Pudding . . . be still my heart. Elsewhere her California spin on Southern classics is equally, ridiculously, good: Deviled Eggs with Smoked Salmon. A vibrant Squash Salad with Pistachios.

Did you know 99 percent of the nation's pistachio orchards are in California? Me neither. Likewise, Steph puts a fresh, herb-y spin on the standby coleslaw. The salads may be prepped ahead and assembled the day of. The chicken is fried once and then fried again early the morning of. This meal is everything everybody loves, and just a little bit better.

Spicy Melon Soup

Serves 6

Refreshing and not too sweet, this Spicy Melon Soup brings raves when we serve it in high summer, when the melons are ripe and it's too hot to cook. Any mix of melon will do, but the watermelon, cantaloupe, and honeydew used here give a nice blend of brightness, flavor, and creaminess respectively. While you are prepping the melon into 1-inch pieces for the blender, cut some extra ¼-inch cubes for the garnish. This is best prepared the same day.

4 cups (1-inch) cubed watermelon
2 cups (1-inch) cubed cantaloupe
2 cups (1-inch) cubed honeydew
1 serrano chili, seeded and chopped
1 lime, juiced
1 cup coconut milk or half-and-half
¼ cup chopped cilantro
2 tablespoons chopped mint, plus extra for garnish
2 tablespoons chopped basil, plus extra for garnish
½ teaspoon salt

Place the melons, serrano, lime juice, and coconut milk into a blender or food processor. Blend at high speed for 30 to 60 seconds or until completely pureed. Add the cilantro, mint, basil, and salt, and pulse 2 or 3 times to blend. Chill completely for at least 1 hour and garnish with chopped herbs and small melon cubes.

Stand-by Hors d'Oeuvres: Pickled Okra and Peanuts

Talk O' Texas Pickled Okra from the grocery store (or www.talkotexas.com) is a standby for us, and I like to have small bowls sitting about on the bar and on occasional tables. Alongside the okra I'll have Aunt Ruby's Peanuts (www.auntrubyspeanuts.com), which I order from the small family-owned company in Enfield, North Carolina, just a few miles from my hometown of Tarboro, where, by the way, my family still grows peanuts. My mother used to fry peanuts, and they were as good as it got. Aunt Ruby's Peanuts are baked, not fried, and for the life of me they are as good as Mama's, which I do not say lightly.

Summer Squash Salad
with Pistachios, Apricots, and Goat Cheese
Serves 6

Choose small zucchini or other squashes; a variety makes a nice contrast in the salad.

1 pound zucchini and/or other small squash varieties,
    if desired
1 teaspoon salt
1 lemon, juiced
2 tablespoons chopped dried apricot
1 slice stale bread, crumbled
4 tablespoons olive oil, divided
1 cup dill sprigs
1 cup mint leaves
1 cup parsley leaves
½ cup roasted pistachios, roughly chopped
3 ounces goat cheese, crumbled

Preheat the oven to 350°F.

Cut the squash into a variety of small bite-size shapes. Place in a large bowl and stir in the salt, lemon juice, and apricots. Cover and refrigerate for at least 30 minutes.

Toss the bread crumbs with 1 tablespoon of olive oil and spread on a baking sheet. Bake for 10 to 12 minutes or until golden brown. Remove from the oven and cool.

To the squash add the dill, mint, parsley, pistachios, and 3 tablespoons olive oil. Add a bit more salt if needed, and spoon onto a serving platter or individual plates. Garnish with the goat cheese and toasted bread crumbs.

Note: Crumbled feta cheese can be substituted for the goat cheese.

The Best Way to Boil an Egg
Place eggs in a saucepan and cover with water ½ inch above the eggs. Bring to a boil, reduce the heat to low, and cook for 8 minutes. Remove from the heat and rinse under cold water continuously for 1 minute. Crack the egg shells and peel under cool running water. Slightly older eggs are easier to peel than fresh ones.

Deviled Eggs
with Smoked Salmon
Makes 12

These Deviled Eggs with Smoked Salmon are a twist on a beloved old favorite and have a yummy surprise of smoked salmon salad at the bottom that is hinted at by the strip of smoked salmon on the top. If you want to cut corners, a simple strip of smoked salmon atop any deviled egg lends an elegant little extra. The recipe is easily doubled or tripled for a crowd.

Deviled Eggs
6 large eggs, hard boiled and peeled
¼ cup Basic Homemade Mayonnaise (page 42)
1½ teaspoons yellow mustard
2 teaspoons lemon juice, divided
Salt and pepper
¼ cup chopped smoked salmon
2 teaspoons drained chopped capers
1 teaspoon chopped parsley
2 teaspoons olive oil
12 (½ x 2-inch) strips smoked salmon
2 teaspoons chopped chives, for garnish
1 teaspoon paprika, for garnish

Slice the boiled eggs in half lengthwise and remove the yolks to a medium mixing bowl. Mash the yolks into a fine crumb using a fork or by pressing through a sieve. Add mayonnaise, mustard, 1 teaspoon lemon juice, salt, and pepper, and mix well.

In a separate small bowl, stir together the chopped salmon, capers, parsley, and olive oil. Stir in the remaining teaspoon of lemon juice and a dash of pepper.

Spoon 1 teaspoon of salmon mixture into each egg white half, then mound a spoonful of the yolk mixture on top. Top the egg with a ½-inch wide strip of smoked salmon and sprinkle with chives and paprika.

Fried Chicken, Extra Crispy

2 chickens yield 16 pieces

This fried chicken recipe is adapted from Saveur Magazine and is the best we've found. A Southern classic, it's become a favorite in our California household and our friends love it. It's also great for a crowd because it's just as good at room temperature. The secret to the juiciness is the brining, and the secret to the crispness is the double frying. Now you know.

Is it us or are chicken breasts channeling Dolly Parton these days? We like cutting those gigantic whole breasts into 4 (or more) pieces to decrease the portion sizes and cooking time vis à vis the other pieces. It also gives those wanting both white and dark meats a less piggy-looking option.

2 whole chickens, cut up
1–4 quarts vegetable oil as needed for frying

For the brine

6 cups water, divided
¼ cup salt
4 tablespoons brown sugar
Spices such as bay leaf, allspice, clove, peppercorns, red chili flakes

For the batter and frying

4 cups flour
2 tablespoons granulated garlic
1½ tablespoons granulated onion
1½ teaspoons cayenne pepper (or to taste)
1 teaspoon paprika
1 teaspoon pepper
1 teaspoon salt
1 tablespoon baking powder
2 teaspoons Tabasco sauce, if desired
2 cups water

For the brine: Bring 2 cups of water to a boil with the salt, sugar, and spices, stirring to dissolve. Remove from the heat and let sit for 15 minutes, then add the additional 4 cups of water. When cool, pour over chicken and refrigerate for at least 3 hours. Remove and pat dry.

Make the batter and fry: Fill a 12-inch cast iron skillet halfway with oil, about 3 cups, and heat to 300°F. Or preheat 4 quarts of oil in a fryer to 300°F.

While the oil is heating, combine the flour, spices, salt, and pepper for the batter mixture and pour half into a bowl and half into a shallow dish or pie plate. To the half in the bowl, whisk in the baking powder and then stir in the Tabasco and water until just mixed.

Dredge chicken in the dry flour mixture, then the wet batter, then the dry mixture again, and carefully lower into the hot oil. Working in batches, fry for 3 to 4 minutes per side. Drain on paper towels.

After the first fry is done, bring the oil temperature to 350° degrees and fry the chicken again in batches for another 2 to 3 minutes per side until golden brown and cooked through. Be careful not to crowd the frying pan, and add oil as needed to keep the oil halfway up the side of the pan.

Drain on paper towels and sprinkle with salt and pepper.

Grilled Pimento Cheese Sandwiches

Makes 2½ cups

Pimento Cheese is in a Southerner's DNA, but it is rapidly catching on elsewhere. As a party starter, on a grilled sandwich, or as a snack, it is simple to make and keeps well in the fridge. Adding a chopped roasted pepper (or two) is optional, but we like the heat. Variations for pimento cheese are many. For a creamier and more spreadable consistency, add some cream cheese, but caution: It's a give-away you are not a Southerner.

Smoked gouda is good to combine with or replace the cheddar, and chopped, roasted jalapeño or habanero picks up the heat. You can also add bacon, herbs, and other spices.

2 cups sharp cheddar cheese, grated
1 (2-ounce) jar pimentos, drained and chopped
¼–½ cup mayonnaise
1 tablespoon grated or finely chopped onion
1 teaspoon Worcestershire sauce
½ teaspoon dry mustard
¼ teaspoon cayenne
6 drops Tabasco
1 roasted jalapeño or fresh habanero pepper, seeded and chopped (optional)

Combine all ingredients in a 2-quart bowl.
Serve at room temperature. Will keep for 2 weeks in the refrigerator.

To make mini grilled cheese sandwiches: Use miniature "party" rye, pumpernickel or other, or regular size loaf bread with the crusts removed and cut diagonally into quarters. Spread or layer the cheese as usual. Melt ½ to 1 tablespoon butter in a skillet over medium-high heat until sizzling, and brown the sandwiches in batches, pressing down lightly with a spatula for a minute or two on each side. Before each batch, add a bit more butter to the skillet and allow it to sizzle.

Basic Homemade Mayonnaise

Makes 1½ cups

Any vegetable oil will work in the mayonnaise recipe. We use half extra-virgin olive oil and half grapeseed oil. Some people find 100% olive oil is heavy, but it is a matter of taste. Very slowly dripping in the oil in the beginning is key to the glorious emulsion of homemade mayonnaise. Thereafter, pour a thin steady stream. Don't glug it in too quickly or the mayonnaise will "break" and there is no saving it. From this basic recipe may be created variations for sauces with herbs, garlic, anchovy, lemon . . .

1 egg
2 tablespoons water
1 clove garlic, chopped
2 teaspoons lemon juice
1 teaspoon Dijon mustard
¼ teaspoon cayenne
¾ cup oil, any vegetable oil will work
1 teaspoon salt
¼ teaspoon pepper

In a blender, combine the egg, water, garlic, lemon juice, Dijon, and cayenne. With the blender running, very slowly drizzle in the oil. When it begins to emulsify, keep pouring in a thin steady stream. Season with salt and pepper. Add a bit more water to thin or a bit more oil to thicken.

Pretend Homemade Mayonnaise

Nothing is better than homemade mayonnaise but if I am too lazy to make it or am short on time, I do this. It's delicious, I swear. Lighten up on the olive oil and lemon juice if you want a firmer consistency. People are particular about their mayonnaise, but it's a fighting word to a Southerner. If there isn't homemade (what?!), most (including me) swear by Hellman's, unless they are from Virginia, in which case it's Duke's. West of the Rockies, Hellman's is supplanted by Best Foods. The Best Foods company bought Hellman's in 1932, but by then both companies made a popular mayonnaise, so they kept both brands.

Whisk together:
1 cup prepared mayonnaise
2 tablespoons olive oil
1 tablespoon lemon juice
1 garlic clove, minced
Pinch of cayenne pepper

Pickled Okra—storebought Talk o' Texas brand—is one of our staple Southern hors d'oeuvres, and no one knows quite how to eat them. Answer: Eat the whole thing, stem end and all. So tangy and good, and perfect with grilled pimento cheese sammies. Custom cocktail napkins are a nice touch and can usually be done in a few weeks' time by your local stationer. (Thank you, Honey Paper in Los Olivos!)

Corn-Bacon-Cheese Muffins

Makes 24 mini muffins or 12 regular muffins

These buttery, bacon-y, cheesy muffins are tender and delicious. We like to bake these in miniature muffin tins, that way everyone can have 2 or 3. Save the fat when you cook bacon and use it in this and other recipes.

1½ cups finely ground cornmeal
1½ cups all-purpose flour, or whole wheat pastry flour
4 teaspoons baking powder
1 teaspoon salt
1 tablespoon sugar
1¾ cups buttermilk
¾ cup butter or bacon fat or a mixture of the two, melted
2 eggs, lightly beaten
1½ cups grated cheddar cheese
½ cup chopped scallions
1 cup crumbled cooked bacon

Preheat oven to 425°F. Grease the muffin tins.

In a large bowl whisk together the cornmeal, flour, baking powder, salt, and sugar. In a separate bowl, whisk together the buttermilk, melted butter and/or bacon fat, and eggs. Quickly and with few strokes stir the wet ingredients into the dry. Then gently fold in the cheese, scallions, and bacon.

Spoon into greased muffin tins, filling about ¾ full, and bake for 15 minutes or until the top springs back when touched.

Coleslaw
with Fresh Herbs

Serves 10

The caraway seeds add an unusual and interesting flavor to the slaw, but if you don't have them in your pantry, leave them out.

3 tablespoons apple cider vinegar
1 tablespoon sugar
¼ cup mayonnaise
1 teaspoon whole caraway seeds
1 head green cabbage, finely shredded
¼ head purple cabbage, finely shredded
1 carrot, shredded
6 scallions, chopped, white and green parts
1 cup chopped herbs such as any combination of
    cilantro, basil, parsley, mint, and dill
Salt and pepper to taste

In a small bowl whisk together the vinegar, sugar, mayonnaise, and caraway seeds. In a large bowl, toss the cabbages, carrots, scallions, and herbs. Pour the dressing over and stir well to combine. Adjust seasoning, cover, and refrigerate for an hour before serving.

Butterscotch Banana Pudding

Serves 10

Because nothing says "Southern" like Banana Pudding, and not to brag, but this rich butterscotch pudding makes this the best one ever, period. To streamline, skip the meringue and top with whipped cream, which is sublime as is.

Note: Cream that is pasteurized as opposed to ultra-pasteurized tastes and whips better.

3 cups heavy cream
1½ cups whole milk
½ vanilla bean, scraped
1 cup + 2 tablespoons packed dark brown sugar
1½ teaspoons salt
½ cup water
1 egg
3 egg yolks
5 tablespoons cornstarch
5 tablespoons butter
1 tablespoon vanilla extract
3–4 bananas, in ¼-inch slices
About 3 cups vanilla wafers
Meringue topping (recipe below)

In a medium saucepan over medium heat, add the cream, milk, and vanilla bean scrapings and pod.

In another medium saucepan combine the brown sugar, salt, and the water. Bring to a boil, reduce the heat and continue cooking until you have a dark caramel with glassy bubbles forming, about 10 minutes.

Meanwhile whisk together the egg, yolks, and cornstarch and set aside.

To the boiling caramel, gradually stir in the cream mixture and return to a boil.

Temper the yolk mixture (and avoid cooking the eggs) by stirring in about a half-cup of the hot caramel-cream mixture, and then add the yolk mixture back into the hot caramel-cream mixture. Continue stirring with a wooden spoon over medium heat until the mixture comes to a boil, about 2 to 3 minutes, then cook for about 30 seconds more and remove from heat. Stir in the butter and vanilla.

In a 12-inch round serving bowl, make 4 layers beginning on the bottom with pudding, then cookies, then bananas, then pudding. Place a layer of plastic wrap directly onto the surface of the pudding to avoid a skin forming. Chill for at least 2 hours or overnight.

Note: Chill a hot mixture quickly by pouring it into a metal or glass container partly submerged in an ice-water bath.

Meringue Topping

4 egg whites (½ cup) at room temperature
Pinch of salt
¾ cup sugar

Whip the egg whites and salt on medium high speed until frothy. While beating, add the sugar 1 tablespoon at a time and beat until thick and glossy.

Spoon or pipe the meringue onto the cooled pudding and either place under a preheated broiler to brown or use a kitchen blow torch to toast the meringue just before serving.

Chocolate Brownies

Makes 1 (8-inch) pan

These brownies are easy, gluten-free, and a delicious step beyond basic brownies, not that we ever met one we didn't like. The almond flour and coconut sugar do lend a special, subtle flavor, but regular white sugar and all-purpose flour may be substituted. Be careful not to overbake.

6 ounces bittersweet chocolate
6 tablespoons unsalted butter
½ teaspoon salt
¾ cup coconut sugar (or regular white sugar)
2 eggs
1 teaspoon vanilla
1 cup almond flour (or regular all-purpose flour)
1 cup chopped nuts
Powdered sugar, if desired

Preheat the oven to 325°F.

Line the bottom of an 8-inch square pan with parchment or wax paper and butter the sides of the pan.

Combine the chocolate, butter, and salt in a double boiler set over simmering water and heat just until the chocolate is melted. Remove from heat and let cool for five minutes before stirring in the sugar, then the eggs and vanilla. Stir in the flour and nuts. Spread into the prepared pan and bake for 15 to 18 minutes. Remove from the oven and cool. Sprinkle with powdered sugar if desired.

Optional: For a quick frosting, combine ¼ cup soft butter with 1½ cups powdered sugar, a few tablespoons of milk, and 4 tablespoons cocoa powder. Melted bittersweet chocolate can also be added to the frosting. Oh, and a pinch of salt. Always a pinch of salt.

Menu

Bagna Cauda

Roasted Porkchops
with Anchovy Aioli and Mint

Farro
with Lemon and Herbs

Honey Cake
with Sautéed Apples

Chapter 4
In the Vineyard

This gathering came together last minute, when I wanted to do *something*, but not much. We were at the tail end of a big weekend and I just didn't have the bandwidth for much more. Table décor needn't be elaborate to be effective. A single element used *en masse* is always striking. You don't even have to use flowers, but some kind of greenery—something living—literally brings life to the table.

A simple ol' picnic table is sturdy and versatile. I prefer those with the benches separate rather than attached, giving you the option to use your own chairs and to use the benches for something else, like a shelf for the ice chest and other service items. The large metal lanterns originally purchased to light an outdoor pathway made a bold statement on the rustic tabletop and worked well in terms of size and scale. The vineyard in autumn is so beautiful that not much else is required. An earth-toned cotton damask tablecloth and napkins were a good background for fall foliage and golden grapevines. To this I added some—gasp—faux bittersweet, which I love and which has managed not to invade our part of California. So sue me, but there is some very good faux flora on the market these days, and I don't mean your grandmother's silk flowers. A bit here and there, every now and then, mixed in with real stuff, I think is okay. I never thought I'd say that, but there you go.

One of the things that most strikes me about the Santa Ynez Valley landscape is that it resembles the South of France and the hills of Tuscany. The climate, topography, and vegetation are all similar, and so naturally it stirs the appetite for similar

cuisines. Olives and olive oil, a bounty of vegetables and herbs, honey, and of course, an abundance of wine.

Even though Bagna Cauda is Italian for "hot bath," the first and unforgettable time I tasted it was in France, years ago in a small country inn near the village of Megève. The fullness of flavors in these simple ingredients is nothing short of voluptuous. The pork chops may be served hot off the grill but both they and the farro are as tasty at room temperature as they are hot, making them a good choice for an al fresco meal, particularly if there is a nip in the air. The densely moist honey-and-apple cake tastes like heaven and will have you leaping for a piece the next morning, if any is left. This is such a simple menu but greatly varied in the kinds of vegetables you can use, and be sure to have a good crusty baguette or sourdough loaf for dipping in the sublime bagna.

It is always a good idea to have wine and pitchers of water directly on the table, and to encourage guests to help themselves. Footmen are scarce these days, and it is tiresome to wait for someone to pour when your glass is empty. As hostess you want to keep the flow going, in every way.

Bagna Cauda

Serves 6

Bagna Cauda means "hot bath" in Italian, though I first encountered this warm, luscious anchovy-butter-garlic-infused dip in the south of France. It is traditionally served as an hors d'oeuvre or first course, with cooked or raw vegetables and a good, crusty bread. Set aside fears of anchovies as they are completely dissolved into the olive oil leaving only their rich, briny deliciousness. Refrigerated leftovers will keep for weeks.

½ cup olive oil
12 cloves garlic, minced
1 (3.5-ounce) jar anchovies
¼ teaspoon red chili flakes
½ cup unsalted butter

Warm the olive oil, garlic, anchovies, and red chili flakes in a small pot over very low heat, for 20 minutes, stirring occasionally and mashing the anchovies until they dissolve. Make sure the garlic does not brown and become bitter. Whisk in the butter and serve warm.

I love when hors d'oeuvres double as first courses and decoration. This colorful bounty of fresh vegetables and baguettes needs little embellishment and beautifully conveys a sense of abundance. Abundance is a great word to keep in mind when entertaining.

Roasted Pork Chops
with Anchovy Aioli and Mint
Serves 4

Seasoning the meat ahead dry-brines it and creates an extra juicy cooked chop. The sugar in the salt rub caramelizes as it cooks.

Note: Though perfectly paired with our Farro with Lemon and Herbs (page 56), these juicy pork chops also make a great meal with Pan Fried Potatoes (page 31) and lightly Sautéed Spinach (page 147).

For the pork chops

4 bone-in pork chops, about 12 ounces each and
    ¾-inch thick
Salt and pepper
1 teaspoon brown sugar
4 teaspoons sunflower seeds, lightly toasted
2 tablespoons olive oil
4 sprigs of mint
Anchovy Aioli

One to three hours before cooking, rub the salt, pepper, and brown sugar over the chops. Cover and refrigerate.

Toast the sunflower seeds in a 300°F oven for about 8 minutes, or for 3 or 4 minutes in a dry pan over medium heat. Don't take your eye off them, as they burn easily.

Heat a 12-inch cast iron skillet or grill to high. Rub the pork chops with olive oil. Sear the chops for 5 minutes on each side for medium, moving around in the skillet to prevent burning. Remove the chops to a warmed platter and garnish with mint leaves and sunflower seeds. Spoon the Anchovy Aioli over the top or serve on the side.

Anchovy Aioli

The difference between aioli and mayonnaise is that aioli originated in Provence, and the garlic is pounded to a paste in a mortar and pestle before being whisked into the egg-lemon-oil mixture. The true aioli would also call for 100 percent olive oil, but other oils may be substituted, such as grapeseed or canola.

Using a mortar and pestle, make a paste of 1 garlic clove, chopped, and 6 anchovy fillets, and add to the recipe for Basic Homemade Mayonnaise (page 42), omitting the recipe's garlic as it is already in your anchovy mixture. The aioli will need less salt than the mayonnaise because of the anchovies. Thin with a bit of water to make it more pourable.

Farro with Lemon and Herbs

Serves 4 to 6

Farro is an ancient variety of wheat that is increasingly popular in the United States. Varieties include einkorn, emmer, and spelt, and may be whole, semi-pearled, or pearled. Cooking times vary, so check the cooking instructions on your package. Soaking is not necessary but will reduce the overall cooking time for any variety.

1 cup farro, soaked in water for at least 30 minutes and up to overnight, drained
2 tablespoons olive oil
1 shallot, minced
1 clove garlic, minced
2 tablespoons chopped parsley
2 tablespoons chopped dill
2 tablespoons chopped basil
1 tablespoon butter
2 tablespoons lemon juice
1 teaspoon salt
¼ teaspoon pepper

Place soaked and drained farro in a 2-quart saucepan. Add water so farro is covered by ½ inch, bring to a simmer, and cook until the grain is tender to the tooth but not mushy. Follow package directions, but cooking time is usually about 20 minutes. Drain.

Heat the olive oil in a 10-inch sauté pan over medium-high heat, add the farro, and fry about 5 minutes or until the grains are toasted and browning. Stir in the shallot and garlic and cook for 2 minutes more. Remove from the heat and stir in the herbs, butter, lemon juice, salt, and pepper.

Honey Cake
with Sautéed Apples

Makes 1 Bundt cake

Served with sautéed apples, this rich, moist cake is a versatile dessert and is as good for breakfast the next morning. The whole wheat flour adds a nice nuttiness, but you can use any combination of all-purpose or whole wheat flour, including 100 percent of one or the other.

For the Cake
2 cups all-purpose flour
1½ cups whole wheat pastry flour
1 tablespoon baking powder
1 teaspoon baking soda
1 tablespoon ground cinnamon
½ teaspoon ground cloves
½ teaspoon ground allspice
1 teaspoon salt
1 cup olive oil
1 cup honey
1½ cups sugar
3 whole eggs
1 cup warm coffee
½ cup orange juice
¼ cup whiskey
1 teaspoon vanilla extract
½ cup slivered or sliced almonds

For the apples
3 tablespoons butter
1 teaspoon cinnamon
4 Granny Smith apples, or other tart cooking apple, peeled, cored, and sliced
2 tablespoons sugar

To make the cake: Preheat the oven to 350°F.

Generously butter and flour a non-stick Bundt pan.

In a large mixing bowl whisk together the flours, baking powder, baking soda, cinnamon, cloves, allspice, and salt. Make a well in the center and set aside. In another large bowl whisk together the olive oil, honey, sugar, eggs, coffee, orange juice, whiskey, and vanilla extract. Quickly stir the wet ingredients into the dry and scrape

into the prepared pan. Sprinkle the slivered almonds over the top and bake for 55 to 60 minutes or until a toothpick inserted in the middle comes out clean. Remove from the oven and cool on a rack for 10 minutes, then remove from the pan and cool completely.

To make the apples: Heat a large sauté pan over medium heat, swirl in the butter and cinnamon, add the apples, turn the heat to high, sprinkle in 2 tablespoons of sugar, and shake and stir the pan until the apples are cooked through, about 2 minutes. Spoon a tablespoon or two of apples over each serving of cake.

Menu

~~~~~~~~

Roasted Butter Pecans

JuneBug's Flatbread

Warm Marinated Brussels Sprouts,
Arugula, and Toasted Walnuts

Duck Lasagna

Poached Oranges

Sautéed Broccoli Rabe

Pumpkin Pie
with Hazelnut Cookie Crust
and Chocolate Drizzle

Brown Sugar Tart

Chapter 5
A Grateful Feast

Isn't Thanksgiving the best? Gathering friends and family for the sole reason of sharing our bounty and counting our blessings is as good as it gets. From our first year together at the ranch, His Grace—that's my husband, Tom—and I have hosted Thanksgivings great and small, welcoming guests from all over and best of all, far-flung children and grandchildren. Part of our tradition is some sort of formal acknowledgement of the holiday and its meaning. This might be as simple as saying aloud what we are grateful for, or as complex as a dramatic re-enactment of the historic event itself. Our friend Adam Firestone rose magnificently to the occasion one year in writing a skit, taking outrageous liberties with history and character interpretation, not to mention political correctness, while his Thespian sister Polly Firestone Walker stepped in as costume mistress. It was great fun. A tremendous effort, but great fun. And while not an annual production, there are rumors of a revival . . .

Though I love tradition, I do not feel bound by it. Hence our decision to forgo for purposes of this book the roast turkey, dressing, and other usual suspects—beloved as they are—of the Thanksgiving repast. If this incites a riot at your house, stick to your own script and try this menu another time. But sometimes it is fun to mix it up, and our menu is certainly seasonal in spirit. The duck lasagna is my own recipe, inspired when an Atlanta friend years ago mentioned in passing that it was their family's traditional holiday fare. Poached oranges are an oldie but goody plucked by my mother from the pages of an oldie-goody itself, *The Joy of Cooking.*

The broccoli rabe has a pungency and spice that its more plebian cousin broccoli lacks, and I love it. Tradition returns in the pumpkin pie, but with our California nutty cookie crust and a stream of chocolate sauce. Ditto the usual pecan pie: Ours is a brown sugar tart (thank you, Cousin Alice) and more butterscotch-y and buttery—with a dash of salt, and walnuts, too.

The tables differ from year to year, as I begin with one idea and build a story around that. Giant woven cornucopias often figure into the scheme, as do a brace of stuffed pheasants, and a pair of turkeys in the entry. Another time it was pumpkins as far as the eye could see . . . I painted place cards-cum-menus in a nod to our family's interests, for example a love of shooting one year and contemporary art another. A Magritte-inspired pilgrim I was especially proud of. Because Thanksgiving is so focused around the table, I tend to go slightly overboard. It gives people something to gobble about.

Excellent. Rhyder liked

JuneBug's Flatbread

Makes 18 small flatbreads

Julie "JuneBug" Williamson began working for my husband's family as a teenager babysitting his young children. When she expressed an interest in cooking, and the children were older, the family sent her to cooking school where she earned her stripes as a professional private chef. JuneBug now resides in the Northeast and continues to cook professionally, but the Dittmer family considers her one of us. Visiting one Thanksgiving, JuneBug gifted us with her famous flatbread, as beautiful as it is delicious.

For the Flatbread

1½ cups warm water

1 tablespoon yeast

1 teaspoon sugar

4½ cups all-purpose flour, divided

½ cup medium grind cornmeal

⅓ cup picked rosemary leaves, roughly chopped

1 teaspoon salt

1 teaspoon pepper

For the Garnish

1 red onion, sliced vertically from the top in ⅛-inch wedges, with the root end left intact to hold the slices together

8 tomatillos, thinly sliced *or tomatoes*

1 cup sage leaves

½ cup olive oil   *options:*

1 tablespoon honey   *carmelized onions*

Salt and pepper   *peppers*

In the bowl of a stand mixer fitted with a dough hook, put the warm water, yeast, sugar, and ½ cup flour. Combine and let sit for 10 minutes to activate the yeast. Add 3½ more cups flour, the cornmeal, rosemary, and salt and pepper, and knead with the dough hook on medium speed until a ball forms and pulls away from the sides of the bowl. If the dough is too sticky, slowly add a tablespoon or 2 of flour and continue kneading for 5 minutes. Press the dough into the bowl, cover with plastic wrap, and set aside to rise in a warm dry place, about 1 hour. The dough should double in volume. Once risen, punch down the dough in the middle and re-form into a ball. At this point the dough can be refrigerated until ready to roll.

To roll and garnish: Preheat the oven to 375°F.

Pinch off walnut-size pieces of dough and form into balls. Place on a greased baking sheet and cover lightly with a kitchen towel. Dust your rolling surface with plenty of flour and roll each ball into a very thin 8 x 3-inch oval and place onto a separate baking sheet. Brush with olive oil and decorate with 1 or 2 slices of red onion and tomatillo. Dab the back side of 3 sage leaves with honey and press into the dough oval. Sprinkle the flatbreads liberally with salt and pepper. Bake for 15 to 18 minutes or until golden brown. Continue rolling and baking in batches, letting the baking sheet cool completely before each use.

Duck Lasagna

Serves 6 to 12, depending on appetites and menu

This duck lasagna has been a go-to for me for years, and I was happy to introduce it to the ranch. It is inspired by an Atlanta friend and chef who proffered it as a Thanksgiving alternative. Rich, flavorful, and festive. No need to cook the lasagna noodles in advance, as they cook in the sauce while baking. And because the sauce is so intensely flavored, it's not a crime in my book to use prepared béchamel (it is, however, a crime in Stephanie's book). Duck confit may be ordered from D'Artagnan, www.dartagnan. com, or Maple Leaf Farms, www.mapleleaffarms.com. If you cannot find dried porcini, use dried shiitakes or a cup of fresh, chopped mushrooms of any variety. This dish may be prepared ahead and frozen, preferably un-baked.

Duck Filling

¼ cup olive oil

1 medium onion, chopped

2 cloves garlic, chopped

1 stalk celery, chopped

1 carrot, chopped

4 whole legs of duck confit (about 8 ounces each),
    skinned, boned, and shredded

1 ounce dried porcini mushrooms, crumbled or chopped

1 cup red wine

1 (16-ounce) can of tomatoes with their liquid

1 cup chicken stock

Béchamel

3 cups whole milk

5 tablespoons butter

6 tablespoons flour

2 teaspoons salt

¼ teaspoon nutmeg

Pasta and Cheese

¾–1 pound of pasta sheets or lasagna noodles

1 cup grated Parmesan cheese, plus extra for serving

For the duck filling: In a large, heavy pan over medium heat, cook the onion, garlic, celery, and carrot with olive oil until softened, 6 to 7 minutes. Add the duck, mushrooms, wine, tomatoes, and stock, and bring to a boil. Reduce heat, cover, and simmer 1 hour, stirring occasionally. Remove cover and simmer another 30 minutes, stirring occasionally until thick. Season with salt and pepper, and skim the fat if desired.

For the Béchamel: In a small saucepan over low heat, warm the milk, being careful not to let it boil or scald. Meanwhile, in a separate medium saucepan over medium heat, melt the butter. Add flour and stir constantly until smooth and light golden brown, 6 to 7 minutes. Gradually stir in the hot milk one cup at a time, whisking continuously until smooth. Bring to a low boil and continue to cook about 3 minutes, continuing to stir. Remove from heat and season with salt and nutmeg.

To assemble and bake: Preheat the oven to 375°F. Grease a 9 x 13-inch baking pan or a 14-inch lasagna pan with oil or butter. Layer from the bottom: duck, pasta, béchamel, cheese. Repeat. Bake 35 to 40 minutes, and let stand for 10 minutes before cutting. Serve with grated cheese on top.

Previous spread: I love painting menu folders that double as place cards. This silly take on Magritte's famous Man in the Bowler Hat *is copied onto 8.5 x 11 watercolor paper and folded over, with the menu cut and pasted inside. Names were penned on the collar. On the mantel, in and around rattan pumpkins and cornucopias (from Pottery Barn) are an array of fresh pumpkins, oak branches, and eucalyptus. The pumpkins eventually make their way to Betsy Bloomingdale, my friend Renee's pet cow.*

Roasted Butter Pecans

Makes 2 cups

The slow baking time allows the butter and seasonings to meld into the pecans.

2 tablespoons butter, room temperature
¾ teaspoon salt
½ teaspoon sugar
½ teaspoon smoked paprika
¼–½ teaspoon cayenne pepper
2 cups raw pecan halves

Preheat the oven to 275°F.

Blend the butter, salt, sugar, smoked paprika, and cayenne together, then massage the mixture into the pecans with your fingers. Place in an even layer on a parchment-lined tray and bake for 20 minutes. Serve warm from the oven, or allow to cool and store in an airtight container for up to a week. These also freeze well.

Poached Oranges

Serves 8

A pretty and perfect companion to any rich meat dish, these poached oranges are easy and different—so different in fact that first-time guests don't quite know what to do with them. They are meant to be eaten with a knife and fork, rind and all. Absolutely delicious and one of my mother's favorites, as was the 1963 Joy of Cooking, from which this recipe derives.

4 navel oranges, cut in half or in thick slices
1 cup sugar
1½ cups water
3 tablespoons lemon juice

Bring a pot or kettle of 5 to 6 cups of water to boil. Place oranges in heavy saucepan on the stove and pour over them enough boiling water to cover and bring to boil. Lower heat and simmer 1 hour and drain well, discarding the water. Return pot to burner on medium heat and cook the oranges 5 minutes more. Remove the oranges and set aside. In the same pot, over medium heat, stir the sugar, 1 ½ cups water, and lemon juice together until the sugar is dissolved. Place the oranges in the syrup, cover, and cook until the oranges are fork tender, about another hour. Refrigerate until serving.

Warm Marinated Brussels Sprouts, Arugula, and Toasted Walnuts

Serves 4 to 6

We love Brussels sprouts and this warm salad is different and divine. The recipe comes from a 1992 issue of the erstwhile, beloved Gourmet *magazine, which I miss, don't you? If absent the luxury of fresh produce, I've made this many times with frozen Brussels sprouts and it is just fine.*

NUTS! They do go bad. Make sure yours are fresh before using them in a recipe.

½ cup lemon juice
½ cup olive oil
1 teaspoon celery salt
Dash of cayenne pepper
1 teaspoon crushed garlic
Dash of Angostura bitters
1 pound Brussels sprouts, steamed and cut in half
1 bunch arugula
½ cup chopped walnuts, lightly toasted

Combine the lemon juice, olive oil, celery salt, cayenne pepper, crushed garlic, and bitters, and pour over the warm Brussels sprouts. Combine with the arugula, or serve mounded over a bed of arugula, and sprinkle with toasted walnuts.

The original recipe also suggested trying with a dash of cloves, Worcestershire sauce, or Pickapeppa sauce. A bit of crumbled bacon is a nice addition, too, but it is delicious as is.

Sautéed Broccoli Rabe

Serves 6 to 8

Broccoli rabe is known for its bright peppery flavor and robust stems. We favor cooking it al dente to preserve its flavor and nutrients, but the brief cooking time leaves the stems a bit tough for the casual dinner knife's cutting power. Hence we suggest trimming to fork-friendly 2-inch pieces. You can cook any vegetable in this manner. The bit of water steams the broccoli at the end. Careful not to burn the garlic and shallot.

2 bunches broccoli rabe
3 tablespoons olive oil
1 shallot, minced
1 clove garlic, minced
1 pinch red chili flakes
½ teaspoon salt
¼ teaspoon pepper

Trim the broccoli rabe to 2-inch pieces, discarding the tough stems. Heat the olive oil in a 12-inch sauté pan over medium-high heat. Add the shallot, garlic, and red chili flakes, and cook just until the garlic starts to brown. Add the broccoli rabe and 3 to 4 tablespoons of water and heat through, stirring and shaking the pan for about 3 minutes, then season with salt and pepper.

Pumpkin Pie
with Hazelnut Cookie Crust and Chocolate Drizzle
Makes 1 (10-inch) pie

Best to make a day ahead to allow time to chill. We generally make this with hazelnuts, but pecans or almonds will do as well. You may omit the ladyfingers but they do add a little tiramisu-like layer of interest. Recipe for Chocolate Sauce follows.

For the crust
8 tablespoons butter, divided
½ cup hazelnuts, pecans, or almonds, toasted
¾ cup all-purpose flour
6 tablespoons sugar
½ teaspoon salt

For the filling
6 egg yolks
6 tablespoons sugar, divided
2 (8-ounce) containers mascarpone, at room
  temperature
1 cup pumpkin puree
¼ cup Grand Marnier
12 ladyfingers
1 cup heavy whipping cream
⅓ cup chocolate sauce (recipe follows)

For the crust: Preheat the oven to 375°F.

Use 2 tablespoons of butter to generously grease a 10-inch pie plate.

Process the toasted nuts in a food processor until fine, but not a paste, about 1 minute. Add the flour, sugar, and salt, and whir until blended. Melt the remaining 6 tablespoons butter and add to the bowl; pulse until just combined and the consistency of wet sand. Press all but ¼ cup of the crust firmly and evenly over the bottom and up the sides of the pie dish. Press the reserved ¼ cup of crust mixture onto a parchment lined baking sheet (this will be crumbled later for the topping). Bake the crust 12 to 15 minutes, until just browned at the edges. Remove from the oven and cool completely. Crumble and set aside the ¼ cup batch.

For the filling: Beat the yolks with 3 tablespoons of the sugar until thick and pale in color, about 5 minutes. Blend in the mascarpone and pumpkin puree. In a shallow bowl stir together the Grand Marnier and 1 tablespoon of sugar, and soak the ladyfingers in the liqueur. Into the baked and cooled pie crust, spread half of the pumpkin mixture, and layer over with the ladyfingers (if using). Spread on the remaining pumpkin mixture and refrigerate at least 6 hours or overnight.

Whip the heavy cream with 2 tablespoons of sugar until soft peaks form, and spread over the pie. Drizzle with chocolate sauce and sprinkle with the reserved crumbled crust. Serve with more chocolate sauce on the side if you like.

Chocolate Sauce
Makes about 2 cups

We prefer the alkalized Dutch process cocoa powder for this silky rich Chocolate Sauce because it is less acidic than natural cocoa powder and has an earthier flavor, but the natural cocoa powder will work as well.

½ cup sugar
½ cup cocoa powder
½ cup honey, agave, or corn syrup
½ cup cream
½ cup water
2 tablespoons butter
½ cup semi-sweet or bitter-sweet chocolate chips

In a 2-quart saucepan over medium-high heat, mix the sugar, cocoa, honey or syrup, and cream with ½ cup water and bring to a boil. Reduce the heat and simmer for 2 to 3 minutes. Stir in the butter and chocolate chips until melted. Store in a heatproof glass container for easy reheating in a microwave or makeshift double boiler. Will keep for several weeks in the refrigerator and may be thinned with a bit of water.

Brown Sugar Tart

Makes a 10-inch tart

This delectable tart originated as individual small brown sugar tarts that were a favorite of my mother's, who got the recipe from our cousin Alice, an ace hostess who also had a very good cook named Georgiana. Truth to tell, I'm guessing Georgiana is the true source for this recipe. The original does not contain nuts, but we like the bit of texture they add and prefer walnuts to the traditional pecans, though you may substitute pecans of course. You may also use a regular pie pan if you don't have one with removable sides.

½ cup butter, room temperature

1 cup dark brown sugar

½ cup white sugar

½ teaspoon salt

2 eggs, beaten

2 tablespoons lemon juice

1 tablespoon flour

1 teaspoon vanilla extract

1 cup chopped walnuts (or pecans)

1 tart crust (recipe on page 33), baked at 350°F degrees
    for 10 minutes

In a large bowl, cream the butter, brown and white sugars, and salt on medium speed for about 5 minutes, until light and fluffy. Mix in the eggs, and stir in the lemon juice, flour, and vanilla. Spread the walnuts (if using) over the pre-baked crust and pour the filling over. Bake on a foil-lined tray for 25 to 30 minutes, or until the center of the tart is firm when shaken. Let cool for 10 minutes then remove the sides of the tart pan.

Serve warm or at room temperature with whipped cream or the Vanilla Ice Cream from page 22.

Menu

Chickpea Soup

Veal Milanese
with Arugula, Tomato,
Mozzarella Salad

Chocolate Cookie
Semifreddo

Chapter 6
A Night at the Opera

We didn't know quite what we were getting into when we agreed to host "A Night at the Opera" to benefit our local St. Mark's Episcopal Church. As the church is very much integrated into all walks of Valley life, including as host for our local Jewish community's services, its programs benefit a diverse population and its activities are widely supported. Hence the enthusiastic embrace of our opera night at about twice the number we had anticipated. Well, the more the merrier, we said. Silently I thought, goodness gracious where am I gon' put all those people?

Meanwhile, back at the ranch (I've been dying to say that), we scrambled. Normally I prefer to avoid removing furniture when entertaining at home so as to preserve the "homeness" but there are times when practicality rules the day, and this was one of them. We have a number of tables and chairs on hand, and best of all a few able-bodied and good-natured fellows to help move them (Wyatt, Juan, and Maestro, here's looking at you!).

Cerulean tablecloths went well with the room and were a compliment to the flowers in vibrant Western sunset hues. We rented bamboo ballroom chairs in lieu of our rather scruffy ladderbacks, and the Mexican tin candlesticks were a sly reference to our region that also lightened the mood of the otherwise serious table setting, and *ecco qua*: Rancho la Scala.

Such a special occasion, we thought, calls for special dress that makes it even more special. Our guests may have been more accustomed to cowboy hats than cufflinks and to boots more than ball gowns, but everyone got into the spirit. His Grace and I got a little silly adding props to our outfits. We were going for a corny sort of Wagnerian-Walkyrie-Brünhilde look, but we looked more like bad extras from *Game of Thrones*, or Game of Thongs, as Tom calls it. Nota bene: the advantage of props over costumes is that props are removable.

The performances were a tour de force. Our town might be small but our talent is not. Soprano Nichole deChaine, tenor Bryan Lane, and accompanist Bev Staples would have been at home on any world stage, but the intimacy of our living room made the experience all the more immediate and engaging. With our senses thus heightened, there was all the more incentive to create a meal that deeply satisfies.

The menu was Italian-inspired and happened to include an all-time ranch favorite, Veal Milanese. It is such a perfect and classic combination of texture, color, and flavor that I cannot resist serving it to our most special guests. The luscious richness of the Chickpea Soup is a gorgeous starter, and the Chocolate Semifreddo hit the perfect sweet note at the end.

Chickpea Soup

Serves 4 to 6

Known as Zuppa de Ceci *in Italian, this is a great soup for a starter or for a quick weeknight dinner.*

2 tablespoons olive oil
½ onion, peeled and chopped
3 cloves garlic, minced
1 small Yukon gold potato, optional
1 (15-ounce) can chickpeas, drained and lightly crushed
Pinch of red chili flakes
3 cups chicken stock or water
1 teaspoon salt
½ teaspoon black pepper
6 tablespoons broken capellini or other tiny pasta
2 tablespoon lemon juice
Chopped parsley or chives

Heat the olive oil over medium-heat in a 4-quart saucepan and stir in the onion and garlic. Cook for 2 minutes, reduce the heat to low, and stir in the potato (if using), and cook 2 minutes more. Add the chickpeas, red chili flakes, chicken stock, salt, and pepper. Bring to a simmer and cook, stirring for 20 minutes. Add the capellini and cook for 8 minutes more. Stir in the lemon juice, adjust the seasoning, and serve with chopped parsley or chives.

Veal Milanese
with Arugula, Tomato, and Mozzarella Salad

Serves 6 or more

As good with chicken as it is with veal, this deeply satisfying one-dish meal has become a mainstay at Rancho La Zaca. It is one of those dishes you can prepare without the recipe once you get the hang of it. Bone-in veal chops are an expensive luxury but make the ultimate, authentic Veal Milanese. If you are using bone-in chops, pound them as close to the bone as you can and cook using 1 pan per chop. The meat may be pounded and breaded several hours in advance, covered, and refrigerated. You may also simplify by preparing the meat as directed and serving with a simple arugula salad, omitting the tomato, mozzarella, onion, and olive.

Veal or Chicken
1½–2 pounds thinly sliced veal cutlets (or 1½–2 pounds chicken breasts), sliced on the bias into 12 (2–3-ounce) cutlets
Salt and pepper
4 whole eggs
6 cups breadcrumbs
3 tablespoons chopped herbs, such as oregano, thyme, and rosemary
3 tablespoons chopped parsley
¾ cup olive oil, divided
8 tablespoons butter, divided
1 lemon, cut into 6 wedges, for serving

Arugula Salad
3 bunches arugula, trimmed and washed
1½ cups mixed herb sprigs such as basil, dill, mint, and chives
3 cups chopped tomatoes, preferably cherry or Roma
12 ounces fresh mozzarella, cubed
1 cup sliced olives (Castelvetrano or Kalamata)
¼ red onion, thinly sliced
Juice of 1 lemon, about 4 tablespoons
6 tablespoons olive oil
Salt and pepper

(Continued on next page)

For the meat: With the flat side of a meat tenderizer, pound the meat cutlets between 2 sheets of plastic wrap or waxed paper to ¼-inch thick. Season with salt and pepper and set aside.

Thoroughly whisk the eggs and pour into a wide shallow bowl or pie plate. On a separate plate, combine the breadcrumbs and herbs. Dredge the meat in the egg and then coat with herbed breadcrumbs on both sides, pressing the crumbs to adhere.

Preheat the oven to 200°F.

Heat 3 tablespoons of olive oil in a 12-inch sauté pans over medium high heat. Put 2 or 3 meat cutlets into the pan. Don't crowd them. Add 2 tablespoon of butter to each pan and cook on one side about 3 minutes until golden brown, then turn and cook on the other side. Transfer to a warm platter or individual plates and hold them in the 200°F oven. Wipe out the pans, then add more olive oil and butter, and continue to cook the remaining meat in batches.

For the salad: While the last round of chicken or veal is cooking, toss together the arugula, herbs, tomato, mozzarella, olives, and red onion. Dress with the lemon juice, olive oil, salt, and pepper. Mound the salad beside or on top of the meat and serve with lemon wedges.

Chocolate Cookie Semifreddo

Serves 8

A divine concoction, semifreddo means half frozen, so it does not harden like ice cream and can be easily sliced or scooped for serving. You will need a candy thermometer, and a hand-held electric mixer is ideal for whipping the egg white mixture.

Note: The semifreddo needs to freeze for at least 3 hours before serving.

8 ounces bittersweet chocolate
4 tablespoons butter, divided
1 cup toasted and peeled hazelnuts
Pinch of salt
1¾ cups heavy whipping cream
1 teaspoon vanilla extract
6 large egg whites
1¼ cups sugar
1–2 cups chopped cookies (any kind)

Brush a 9-inch loaf pan lightly with oil and then line with plastic wrap and set aside.

Melt the chocolate and 2 tablespoons of butter in a large bowl over a double boiler, and set aside to cool.

Process the hazelnuts and 2 tablespoons butter in a food processor to a smooth paste and stir into the cooling chocolate. Add a pinch of salt.

Whip the cream and vanilla to firm peaks and set aside in the refrigerator.

In a clean bowl over a double boiler, combine the egg whites and sugar, whisking continuously until the temperature reaches 140° on a candy thermometer, about 3 to 5 minutes. Remove the bowl, and with an electric mixer, whip on medium-high speed until the meringue forms stiff, glossy peaks, about 12 to 15 minutes.

Fold the cooled chocolate and nut mixture into the whipped cream and then gently fold in ¼ of the meringue. Fold in the remaining meringue along with the chopped cookies.

Scoop into the plastic-lined pan, smoothing down to press out air bubbles. Cover and freeze for at least 3 hours.

To serve, either scoop the semifreddo like ice cream (easier), or invert the pan onto a serving plate and cut into slices with a warm, serrated knife. Serve with Chocolate Sauce (page 66).

In the know on cocoa: Dutch processed or natural?

In a sauce recipe, either Dutch processed or natural cocoa powder can be used. The Dutch is more alkaline and may have an earthier flavor, while the natural is more acidic. But in baking, because alkali and acid react specifically with a recipe's leavening agents (i.e., salt, baking soda, or baking powder) it is best to use the type indicated in the recipe. Our favorite brand of Dutch processed is Valrhona. For natural cocoa powder, we like Dagoba.

Menu

Chilled Cucumber Soup

Olive Oil Poached Halibut
with Sauce Verte

Green Spring Vegetables
with Mint and Dill

Melon Sorbet

Ricciarelli Cookies

Chapter 7
Ladies' Lunch

A "ladies' lunch" sounds almost nostalgic, a special occasion rather than a regular weekday meal. These days it seems that the ladies who could be "ladies who lunch" are too busy being something else. Even life in small country towns like ours seems to brim with commitments that leave little room for a leisurely, midday meal. Perhaps that is why exactly such a meal is a luxury, a gift, and sometimes a moral imperative.

And yet, I sometimes catch myself complaining about having agreed to a lunch, how it wrecks the day, how I could be doing this or that and now cannot, and yadda yadda yadda. You know? Therefore I am as selective about attending a lunch as I am about hosting one, mindful of constraints both timely and caloric. As to menu, particularly at midday, one would like not to feel one has swallowed an elephant. Keep it light. Our chilled

cucumber soup and poached fish with sublime vinaigrette is substantial without being heavy. Melon sorbet is the perfect, fruity finish, and feel free to purchase it if your own time constraints disallow its making at home. Stephanie's friend's ricciarelli cookies were a revelation to me, a sweet treat with sweet story behind them too.

Setting a table in linen and silver is such a pleasure—old-fashioned, a bit prissy, civilized, and satisfyingly atavistic, as I imagine my mother and grandmother using these very things, handed on by their mothers and grandmothers. Setting a table is also setting an intention to gather together and to hear and be heard, to talk about everything and nothing, to indulge in the very sort of aimless and yet purposeful activity that behavioral experts today call "play," and they strongly encourage it. Like play, a lovely lunch with friends can leave us relaxed, refreshed, and reconnected—to ourselves and to one another.

Chilled Cucumber Soup

Serves 4

A flavorful and refreshing cucumber soup that is an ideal first course for a summer meal, and also good as hors d'oeuvres served in demitasse cups. Allow for an hour or more of chilling time before serving, or make it the day before. To boost the chilling on a hot day, put the soup in a metal container and put in a larger bowl of ice water.

3–4 cucumbers (about 3 cups), peeled, seeded, and chopped
1 cup plain yogurt or buttermilk
1 tablespoon lime juice
1 tablespoon chopped basil
1 tablespoon chopped cilantro
1 tablespoon chopped mint
½ teaspoon salt
¼ teaspoon ground black pepper
1 jalapeño, seeded and chopped (optional)

For garnishing
¼ cup chopped red onion
¼ cup chopped cucumber
½ avocado, chopped
Olive oil for drizzling
Chopped cilantro

Combine cucumber, yogurt or buttermilk, and lime juice in the blender and blend well. Add basil, cilantro, mint, salt, pepper, and jalapeño, and blend another 10 to 15 seconds. Chill in the refrigerator for an hour before serving.

Garnish with red onion, cucumber, avocado, a drizzle of olive oil, and chopped cilantro.

Olive Oil Poached Halibut
with Sauce Verte

Makes 4 servings

Any firm fish can be substituted for the halibut. Buy what looks best that day. The poaching oil can be infused with spices and herbs as you like, such as peppercorns, red pepper flakes, and sprigs of mint or dill. Your poaching pot should be large enough to hold the fish in one layer. Leftover bits of poached fish make a lovely salad tossed with Persian cucumbers and cherry tomatoes.

4 (5–6-ounce) halibut filets
Salt and pepper
2 cups olive oil
1 sprig thyme or rosemary
1 clove garlic, peeled

Remove the halibut from the refrigerator 30 minutes before poaching. Sprinkle with 1 teaspoon of the salt and ½ teaspoon of the pepper.

Preheat the oven to 250°F.

In a 12-inch oven-proof pot or pan over medium heat, add the olive oil, the thyme, and clove of garlic, and warm for 5 minutes. Remove from the heat and add the fish. There should be enough oil just to cover. If not, add a bit more. Place the pan in the oven and bake for 10 to 15 minutes or until the fish is just cooked through. While the fish is cooking, make the sauce.

Sauce Verte
A classic and versatile sauce that needs no cooking and is good on so many things, from fish and chicken to beef and vegetables.

1 cup fresh parsley leaves
⅓ cup fresh dill sprigs
⅓ cup fresh mint leaves
¼ cup tarragon leaves
1 small shallot, peeled and minced
1 clove garlic, peeled and minced
1 teaspoon Dijon mustard
2 tablespoons fresh lemon juice
1 tablespoon red wine vinegar
½ cup olive oil
¼ cup capers, drained and chopped

6 anchovy fillets, drained and chopped
Pinch of red pepper flakes
2 teaspoons salt
1 teaspoon pepper

Chop the parsley, dill, mint, and tarragon together and place in a bowl. Add the shallot and garlic to the herbs along with the mustard, lemon, red wine vinegar, and olive oil. Stir in the chopped capers and anchovies. Season with red pepper flakes, salt, and pepper.

On Cooking Fish

The 10-minute rule for cooking fish calls for 10 minutes of cooking time per inch of thickness at the fish's thickest point, turning it halfway through. If the fish is 2 inches thick at its thickest point, you cook it for 20 minutes, and so on. Estimate the in-between sizes. If the fish is ½ inch or less, cook it just a minute or two on the second side. Add 5 minutes if cooking in liquid.

The "snow-cap" of sweetened condensed milk is how they serve shaved ice at beach stands in Hawaii. It adds the perfect hit of sweet and creamy.

Green Spring Vegetables
with Mint and Dill
Serves 6

Lots of chopped fresh herbs highlight the bright green flavors of spring. We've used asparagus and snap peas here but you might also try pea shoots, peas, julienned zucchini, escarole, watercress, snow peas, haricots verts, or any combination thereof.

   Note: The timing on this recipe is for pencil-thick asparagus. Cook less for thinner asparagus and more for thicker. We usually peel asparagus that is thicker than a pencil.

1 pound asparagus
1 pound snap peas
3 tablespoons olive oil
1 shallot, minced
1 clove garlic, minced
¼ cup torn mint leaves
¼ cup chopped dill
1 teaspoon lemon zest, optional
¾ teaspoon salt
¼ teaspoon pepper

Cut the asparagus into ¾-inch lengths. Trim the peas and cut into bite size pieces. Heat a 12-inch sauté pan over high heat, and add the olive oil, asparagus, and peas. Cook for 3 minutes or until the vegetables are starting to soften, then add the shallot and garlic and cook for 2 minutes more. Remove from the heat and stir in the mint, dill, lemon zest, salt, and pepper. Serve hot or at room temperature.

Melon Sorbet
Serves 4

You will need an ice-cream maker for this sorbet. You may substitute any seasonal fruit for the melon and adjust the amount of sugar to taste.

1 small cantaloupe, or 3 cups cubed melon, plus
   4 tablespoons small-diced melon for garnish if desired
⅓ cup water
¼ cup honey or sugar
2 tablespoons lime juice
Pinch of salt
2 tablespoons sweetened condensed milk, optional

Place the melon in a blender with ⅓ cup of water, honey, lime juice, and salt, and blend thoroughly. Freeze according to ice-cream maker directions.

   Scoop sorbet into bowls, top with the small-diced melon and, if you like, a drizzle of sweetened condensed milk.

Ricciarelli Cookies

Makes 3 dozen

Like a macaroon showing off, this almond-y Tuscan cookie has a lightly crisp outside and a luscious chewy inside.

Stephanie created this recipe for her dear friend Monica Rinaldi Semerdjian, who passed away at a young age from a rare and untreatable form of cancer. With six months to live, Monica sent friends a letter with her parting pearls of wisdom. Says Steph, "Monica, as always, you were right: Everyone should try this cookie, print their photos, volunteer, eat farm to table, use snail mail, support local businesses, and feed a friend. Food is so intertwined with our memories and these Ricciarelli cookies always make me smile to think of a friend."

12 ounces blanched or slivered almonds, lightly toasted
1¾ + ¾ cups powdered sugar, divided
Pinch of salt
¼ teaspoon baking powder
1 teaspoon orange zest
3 egg whites, room temperature
1 teaspoon almond extract
1 teaspoon vanilla extract

Preheat the oven to 325°F.

Grind the almonds to a fine meal in a food processor. Add 1¾ cups powdered sugar, salt, baking powder, and orange zest, and whiz until thoroughly combined. Transfer to a large bowl.

In a separate bowl whisk the egg whites to soft peaks and add the almond and vanilla extracts. Fold ⅓ of the whites into the ground almond mixture to lighten it, and then fold in the remaining whites.

Pour the ¾ cup of powdered sugar into a small, shallow dish. Drop small teaspoons of the cookie dough into the sugar. Coat each spoonful of dough evenly with the sugar, form them into small, oblong shapes, and place on a parchment-lined cookie tray about 2 inches apart. Set aside to "dry" for 1 hour before baking.

Preheat the oven to 325°F and bake the cookies for 10 to 12 minutes or until lightly golden brown on the bottom. Cool completely. They will be lightly crisp on the outside and chewy on the inside.

Menu

Cheese Straws

Bacon Crackers

Avocado and Grapefruit Salad
with Marcona Almonds and Mint

Jambalaya

Roasted Tomatoes

Grilled Pineapple
with Brown Butter Ice Cream
and Caramel Sauce

Chapter 8
Ringing in the New

I love spending New Year's Eve at home, whether mine or someone else's. My penchant to avoid the general public on this particular night has never wavered. To all those adventurous souls braving the Times Squares of the world, bless you and be careful. Wherever it is, New Year's Eve does harbor a heightened expectation, if for nothing else than for what awaits us in the year ahead. Such auspiciousness merits recognition.

Beginning with getting dressed. It does not take the keenest observer to note the almost pathological casualness of Californians. I hew to the notion that stepping up one's sartorial game steps it up all around. Even hardcore hoody-wearing Mark Zuckerburg wore a tie to testify before Congress. It's not about money; it's about looking like an unmade bed. So, let's dress up now and then for heaven's sake. "Beauty is truth," said Keats, and he was right.

The tables were dressed up as well. Months before, I had spotted these wonderful Bunny Williams—designed crystal pagodas in the Ballard Designs catalog and snapped them up. They were the touchstone of my design, and I schemed the table around them. Every design needs a touchstone, by the way, an object or idea to build a story around. Sparkle, silver, and gold were the words that came to mind, and I went from there. There was something lovely about the metallic and neutral-toned décor setting off the men's ebony dinner jackets and the ladies' colorful gowns.

With all this fanciness I was inclined to go simple with the menu, which would set a relaxed tone, lest fancy veer to fussy, which I like to avoid in any case

and especially at home. I cannot stand for things to look commercial, cater-y, or store-bought, even if they are. It is home and should look and feel like home, not a restaurant. I also like to serve dishes at home that my guests aren't likely to have everywhere else. The retro-country-club citrus and avocado salad is so delicious in California this time of year, and the perfect foil for a seafood-centric main course. Jambalaya has Southern roots, and its satisfying meld of flavors and textures make it a sure-fire crowd-pleaser. The dessert of grilled pineapple and homemade ice cream is labor intensive but a show-stopper worthy of ringing in the New Year in grand style. You could also serve premium ice cream bars on beautiful plates, alongside dishes of the yummiest cookies and best quality chocolates to be passed around the table. At the risk of contradicting myself (not that it would be the first time), I realize ice-cream bars are by definition "store-bought," but what restaurant, or stuffy hostess for that matter, would serve a store-bought ice cream bar? There you go. Stuffy hostess you are not. Letting yourself off the hook is one of the best New Year's resolutions there is.

Speaking of, guests were asked to bring with them a written intention they wanted to set for the New Year. After dinner, and just before midnight, which at the ranch we celebrate on New York time, we reconvened outside on the porch, where a blazing fire awaited us. Ceremonially we tossed our intentions into the fire, letting go the old-bad and inviting in the new-good. Then we ignited our giant sparklers and welcomed the New Year in laughter and light.

Cheese Straws

Yields 1 pound

Cheese Straws are a classic Southern staple. Alongside Roasted Butter Pecans (page 64), these cheese straws are our go-to hors d'oeuvres combo at the ranch. A cookie press is handy for making cheese straws, but not mandatory.

½ cup unsalted butter at room temperature
3 cups grated sharp cheddar cheese
1½ cups all-purpose flour
1 teaspoon salt
1 teaspoon Worcestershire sauce
½ teaspoon smoked paprika
¼ teaspoon cayenne pepper
¼ teaspoon Tabasco sauce

Preheat oven to 375°F. Line two 10 x 7-inch cookie sheets with parchment paper.

In the bowl of a food processor, blend the butter and cheese to a paste. Add the rest of the ingredients and process just until combined and the dough forms a ball. If using a cookie press, use the star shape hole. Load the dough into the press and pipe onto parchment lined cookie sheets, cutting into 2- or 3-inch lengths. Bake for 10 to 12 minutes or until lightly browned on the bottom.

If not using a cookie press, roll the dough into three 1-inch cylinders, wrap tightly in plastic wrap, and refrigerate for at least 1 hour. Remove the plastic and slice into ¼-inch discs, placing them on a parchment-lined cookie sheet.

Bake for 12 to 15 minutes or until lightly browned on the bottom.

Store in an airtight container for up to 1 week or freeze for up to 6 months.

Bacon Crackers

Makes 30 crackers

Another old-timey Southern favorite, these can be made ahead and frozen. Use regular sliced bacon, not thick cut.

10 slices bacon
30 saltine crackers

Preheat the oven to 375°F.

Cut bacon slices into thirds and wrap around the center of the saltine. Place with the bacon ends facing down on a wire rack set over a baking sheet. Bake for 30 minutes or until the crackers are golden brown and the bacon is cooked through and crispy. The crackers will shrink in the middle as the bacon cooks and contracts.

Jambalaya

Serves 12

For less fancy occasions, we like to serve Jambalaya straight off the stovetop, setting up a buffet on the kitchen island for a cozy, casual supper. It is okay to use frozen, prepared shrimp. If you peel your own shrimp, a recipe for Shrimp Stock follows on this page. Serve with sourdough garlic bread or toasted baguettes.

36 (21/25 count) shrimp, peeled and deveined
1 (3½-pound) chicken, boned, or 2 pounds of boneless
    chicken, cut into 2-inch pieces
3 tablespoons Creole Spice, divided (recipe follows)
4 tablespoon olive oil
2 tablespoons unsalted butter
1 cup coarsely chopped onion
1 green bell pepper, coarsely chopped
1 red bell pepper, coarsely chopped
2 stalks celery, chopped
3 cloves garlic, minced
2¾ cups uncooked long grain white rice
6 Roma tomatoes, peeled, seeded, and chopped,
    or 1 (15-ounce) can whole tomatoes, broken up
2 teaspoons Worcestershire sauce
1½ pounds andouille sausage, sliced
7 cups chicken, shrimp, or other seafood stock
Salt and pepper
4 green onions, white and green parts, sliced for garnish

Season the shrimp and chicken with 2 tablespoons of the Creole Spice, cover the shrimp and refrigerate.

Heat the olive oil in a large pot over medium heat. Brown the chicken on all sides and remove from the pan. To the same pan add the butter, onions, peppers, celery, and garlic and cook, stirring constantly for 10 to 15 minutes. Add the rice and the remaining tablespoon of Creole Spice, stirring thoroughly. Add the tomatoes, Worcestershire, sausage, and stock. Add the chicken back to the pan and bring to a boil. Taste the broth and season with salt and pepper. Cover, reduce heat to low, and cook for 15 minutes. Add the shrimp, stir, cover, and continue cooking another 10 minutes until the shrimp are cooked through.

Sprinkle with the green onion before serving.

Creole Spice

Yields ¾ cup

A spicy wake-up for any soup, stew, or meat seasoning.

3 tablespoons paprika
2 tablespoons smoked paprika
2 tablespoons granulated garlic
1 tablespoon onion powder
1 tablespoon dried oregano
1 tablespoon dried thyme
2 teaspoons cayenne pepper
2 tablespoons salt
1 tablespoon ground black pepper

Combine all ingredients and store in a glass jar. Will keep up to 3 months.

Shrimp Stock

Yields 3 cups

1 tablespoon grapeseed oil
½ cup chopped onion
¼ cup chopped carrot
¼ cup chopped celery
1 clove garlic
2 tablespoons tomato paste
Shrimp shells from 1–3 pounds of shrimp

Heat the oil over high heat in a 4-quart saucepan. Add the onion, carrot, and celery. Cook, stirring occasionally, for 6 minutes or until starting to brown. Add the garlic, cook and stir an additional 2 minutes. Add the tomato paste and cook for 1 minute more. Add the shrimp shells and stir until they turn pink. Cover with water and bring to a boil. Lower the heat and simmer for 30 minutes. Strain. May be frozen for later use.

Roasted Tomatoes

Serves 8 to 10

The smell of roasting tomatoes is intoxicating. Leftovers can be puréed for a quick and full-flavored tomato sauce or frozen for later use in soups and stews—a handy tip for a bumper crop in summer.

8 medium-sized heirloom tomatoes
3 tablespoons olive oil
1 teaspoon salt
½ teaspoon sugar
½ teaspoon pepper
1 tablespoon thyme leaves

Preheat the oven to 400°F.

Cut the stem out of the tomato, trim the bottom, and cut in half. Lay cut side up on a parchment paper–lined baking sheet. Drizzle with olive oil and sprinkle with the salt, sugar, pepper, and thyme. Bake for 25 to 35 minutes until the tomatoes are starting to brown. Best served hot from the oven.

Avocado and Grapefruit Salad
with Marcona Almonds and Mint
Serves 6

Have all the ingredients ready to go and save the avocado until the last minute to keep it from browning.

Note: The easiest way to slice an avocado is to remove the little button of a stem at the top, then cut lengthwise in half, cutting around the pit. Separate the two halves and with the sharp edge of the knife cut into the pit, loosen, and remove it. Use a large spoon to scoop the avocado from the shell and slice or dice as you like.

3 avocados, sliced
3 grapefruits, peeled, segmented, seeds removed
1 bunch watercress or other greens
½ cup mint leaves
6 tablespoons Marcona almonds, chopped or crushed
2 tablespoons lemon juice
4 tablespoons olive oil
Salt and pepper

Divide the avocado and grapefruit among six plates. In a bowl, toss together the greens and mint and mound atop the avocado and grapefruit. Sprinkle on the almonds, drizzle with lemon juice and olive oil, and season with salt and pepper.

Opposite: These Bunny Williams-designed lanterns for Ballard Designs were the inspiration for the sparkly look of the party.

Having a local psychic to tell fortunes for the year ahead was a big hit with guests—even those I didn't think would go in for it. Lots and lots of balloons are an inexpensive and always effective decor element. Helium tanks can be ordered online if you cannot find one locally.

Grilled Pineapple
with Brown Butter Ice Cream and Caramel Sauce
Serves 8

You could try this also with peaches, plums, or nectarines. The fruit can be broiled in the oven as well. Prepared vanilla ice cream and caramel sauce can do in a pinch, of course. In a different pinch, a drizzle of warm honey (as pictured) can replace the caramel sauce.

1 pineapple, peeled, cored, and cut into 8 long wedges
2 tablespoons sugar
½ vanilla bean pod, split and scraped (reserve scrapings)
Brown Butter Ice Cream (recipe below)
Caramel Sauce (recipe below)

Preheat grill to medium high, or oven to broil.

Gently toss the pineapple wedges with the sugar and vanilla bean scrapings and let sit for 10 minutes.

Grill or broil on both sides for 1 minute or until lightly charred.

Remove from the heat and place 1 or 2 spears on each plate. Top with a scoop of ice cream and drizzle of caramel sauce.

Brown Butter Ice Cream
Makes about 2¼ cups
Minus the brown butter flavoring, this basic vanilla recipe can be a base for any flavor of ice cream.

1 cup whole milk
½ cup half-and-half
½ cup cream
6 tablespoons sugar, divided
¼ vanilla bean, split and scraped
4 egg yolks
Pinch salt
1 teaspoon vanilla extract
Brown butter flavoring, if desired (see below)

In a medium saucepan over medium heat, pour the milk, half-and-half, and cream. Sprinkle in 3 tablespoons of sugar and add the vanilla bean and scrapings, but do not stir. Bring to a light simmer.

Meanwhile place the egg yolks in a medium-sized bowl with the remaining 3 tablespoons of sugar and whisk together.

Add a spoonful or two of the hot cream mixture to the yolks to temper them so that they do not cook. Whisking constantly, slowly add the remaining cream mixture to the egg yolks.

Return the combined custard mixture to the pan on medium heat. Stir constantly with a wooden spoon until the mixture starts to thicken and coat the back of the spoon. Immediately pour into a clean bowl in an ice bath to cool.

Season with a pinch of salt and the vanilla extract.

When cool, strain and refrigerate for at least 3 hours.

Freeze according to ice-cream machine directions. When the ice cream is almost finished, slowly stir in the brown butter. Store in the freezer until serving.

To make the brown butter: In a small saucepan over medium-low heat, warm 3 tablespoons of butter until bubbling and golden brown.

Caramel Sauce
Makes ¾ cup

½ cup sugar
¼ teaspoon fresh lemon juice
2 tablespoons water
½ cup heavy cream
2 tablespoons unsalted butter
Pinch salt

In a small saucepan, combine the sugar and lemon juice with 2 tablespoons of water. Stir over medium heat until the sugar has dissolved, then raise the heat to medium high and bring to a boil. Do not stir from this point, but do wash down the sides of the pan with a wet pastry brush to prevent crystallization.

Cook the sugar until it reaches an even, deep brown color, about 12 minutes. Carefully whisk in the cream, butter, and salt, and cook for 1 minute more. Remove from the heat. This can be made several days ahead and refrigerated.

Reheat gently in a double-boiler or in the microwave.

Menu

Watermelon and Tomato Salad

Grilled Chicken & Shrimp Kabobs
with Lemon Yogurt Vinaigrette

Stuffed Grape Leaves

Toasted Pita Chips with Hummus

Deviled Eggs with Anchovy

Freekeh
with Lemon and Herbs

Quinoa
with Citrus Tahini

Fattoush

Pistachio Almond Butter Cake

Chapter 9
A Shooting Party Picnic

Picnics are great because food tastes better outdoors. It just does. Even though all the schlepping and prepping and what-not is kind of a pain, it is such fun in the end. With the availability nowadays of wonderful tin and Melamine plates, bamboo utensils, and other attractive unbreakables, your settings can be quite stylish despite the ruggedness of locale.

It isn't often we have lunch at the Rancho La Zaca shooting range (because like I said, it's kind of a pain) but it is such a treat when we do. The view is glorious and there is the sense of being in another place, like being in the bush, almost. Shooting sporting clays is a favorite activity at the ranch and one we especially like to share with friends. We'll have instructors a couple of times a year and invite the neighbors, usually organizing a gathering around that time, including a spirited competition or two. Despite the macho allure of shooting sports, testosterone *per se* does not confer success. It is a game of finesse, hand-eye coordination, and calm under pressure. In other words, girls can kick ass at it, too, and do. After the scores are tallied, future challenges issued, oaths sworn, and egos bolstered or bruised, the shooting of bull continues with lunch.

Lunch at the range is somewhat a glorified picnic, and a jauntily set table greeting shooters at the end of their rounds is a delightful surprise—even to me, sometimes, as I often don't know what it's going to look like until it is finished, as was the case on this day. Bright dahlias and zinnias from our garden in simple glass bottles were easy to do but made a big visual splash with colorful napkins and pillows nicked from the breakfast room. There is

an outdoor kitchen of sorts, but mostly the meal is prepared at home and toted to range, in true picnic fashion. The menu is one that can be prepared in advance and holds well at room temperature, qualities well suited to Middle Eastern food, which we love and which beautifully comprises the best of California comestibles. Savory kabobs, stuffed grape leaves, hearty grain salads, and pistachio-almond-cake are as satisfying as they are easy to prepare. This is the sort of meal meant to be grazed upon, lingered over, nibbled at, and—forgive the pun—reloaded time and again.

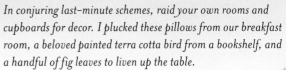

In conjuring last-minute schemes, raid your own rooms and cupboards for decor. I plucked these pillows from our breakfast room, a beloved painted terra cotta bird from a bookshelf, and a handful of fig leaves to liven up the table.

Grilled Chicken & Shrimp Kabobs
with Lemon Yogurt Vinaigrette
Serves 4 to 8

Kabobs can be cooked on the grill or broiled in the oven. If using wooden skewers, soak them in water for at least 30 minutes before grilling. We say this serves 4 to 8 depending on your menu and what else is on offer.

Excellent ✓   *didn't love the vinaigrette*

Grilled Chicken Kabobs

1½ pounds boneless chicken breast cut into ¾-inch
   cubes

3 tablespoons olive oil

1 tablespoon lemon juice

1 tablespoon chopped fresh oregano

1 teaspoon turmeric

½ teaspoon ground cumin

Pinch of cinnamon

1 teaspoon salt

½ teaspoon pepper

Mix together the chicken cubes, olive oil, lemon, oregano, turmeric, cumin, cinnamon, salt, and pepper. Cover, and refrigerate at least 30 minutes or up to overnight. The longer the better. When ready to cook, skewer the chicken and season with salt and pepper.

Preheat a grill to medium-high heat, or preheat the oven broiler and position the rack about 3 inches from the top. If grilling, cook for 8 minutes, turning every 2 minutes. If oven broiling, place kabobs in a pan and cook about 6 minutes, turning every 2 minutes or until done. Serve with Lemon Yogurt Vinaigrette (page 98).

Grilled Shrimp Kabobs
Serves 4 to 8

The 16/20 count shrimp means there are 16 to 20 shrimps per pound. Allow $^1/_3$ to ½ pound of shrimp per person. If you are cleaning the shrimp yourself, reserve the shells to make Shrimp Stock (page 88). The shrimp can be cooked on the grill or broiled in the oven.

Note: Shrimp from Kauai have a sweet, true shrimp flavor. Ask your fishmonger about availability.

1½ pounds (16/20 count) shrimp, peeled
    and deveined
3 tablespoons olive oil
3 tablespoons chopped fresh oregano
1 clove garlic, minced
1 teaspoon smoked paprika
Salt and pepper

Combine the peeled shrimp with the olive oil, oregano, garlic, and smoked paprika. Cover and refrigerate for at least 30 minutes or as long as overnight. The longer the better. When ready to cook, skewer the shrimp, 3 or 4 per skewer, "spooning" them together. Season with salt and pepper.

Preheat the grill to medium, or pre-heat the oven broiler and position the rack 3 inches from the top. Grill the kabobs about 3 minutes per side or until cooked through, or place on a broiler pan and broil for 3 minutes on the first side and 1 minute on the other, just until the shrimp are reddish pink and opaque. Serve with Lemon Yogurt Vinaigrette.

Lemon Yogurt Vinaigrette
Makes 1 cup

With swirls of yogurt and bright yellow olive oil, this dressing is quite pretty. You will want to put this on everything—salads, grains, vegetables, chicken, and fish. Doubles easily and can be made several days ahead.

6 tablespoons olive oil
4 tablespoons lemon juice
4 tablespoons chopped parsley
2 tablespoons chopped dill
1 clove garlic, minced
1 small shallot, minced
$^1/_3$ cup plain Greek yogurt
1 teaspoon salt
½ teaspoon pepper

Whisk together the olive oil, lemon, herbs, garlic, and shallot. Stir in the yogurt, salt, and pepper. Adjust seasoning and refrigerate until you are ready to serve.

Watermelon and Tomato Salad
Serves 6

If preparing ingredients ahead, drain the cut watermelon on paper towels or in a colander.

Persian cucumbers are great as a substitute for the regular variety and there is no need to peel or seed them.

6 cups cubed watermelon
3 cups arugula
1 cup chopped heirloom or cherry tomatoes
1 cup peeled, seeded, and diced cucumber
¼ red onion, thinly sliced
1 heaping tablespoon each basil, mint, and dill,
    leaves picked and torn to small pieces
½ cup chopped Kalamata olives
½ cup crumbled feta cheese
3 tablespoons lemon juice
5 tablespoons olive oil
Salt and pepper to taste

Just before serving, toss all ingredients together in a large bowl, and season with salt and pepper.

A look of abundance is the key to a beautiful (and photogenic) buffet table. Fill in with foliage, flowers, and decorative objects to limit the amount of "table space" showing. You want some space of course, but not too much. Keep in mind which dishes require serving with two hands, and leave space on the buffet for the guest to put down her plate in order to serve.

Fattoush

Serves 6 to 8

A traditional Lebanese bread and vegetable salad, fattoush is fantastic with grilled lamb or chicken. The addition of eggplant elevates the everyday fattoush and takes it somewhere new. This is an excellent method for cooking eggplant for almost anything, by the way. For an inspired mezze, or simple salad, combine cooked eggplant with raw chopped tomatoes to serve with any Mediterranean-style meal.

Croutons

1 large pita bread cut into quarter-size pieces
2 tablespoons olive oil
¼ teaspoon salt

Eggplant

4 tablespoons olive oil, divided
3 small Italian eggplant, or one large eggplant, peeled, diced, salted, and drained in a strainer for 1 hour
1 small onion, diced
1 clove garlic, minced
1 cup sliced olives, such as Kalamata or Castelvetrano
1 tablespoon chopped oregano and/or thyme
2 tablespoons lemon juice
Salt and pepper

Salad

2 heads of Little Gem lettuce or 1 head Romaine, chopped
2 cucumbers, peeled, seeded, and diced
½ pint cherry tomatoes, halved
¼ red onion, thinly sliced
½ cup feta cheese
3 tablespoons olive oil
2 tablespoons lemon juice
¼ cup torn basil leaves
¼ cup torn mint leaves or dill sprigs (optional)
Salt and pepper

For the croutons: Preheat the oven to 350°F.

In a bowl, toss the pita with olive oil and salt and bake for 12 minutes or until crisp. May be made ahead and cooled before adding to the salad.

For the eggplant: Heat a 12-inch sauté pan over high heat and add 2 tablespoons of the olive oil. Squeeze out the excess moisture from the eggplant, and add the eggplant to the pan. Reduce the heat to medium-high and sauté, stirring, for 10 to 12 minutes until the eggplant is browned and cooked through. Add the remaining olive oil, onion, and garlic, and cook 5 minutes more. Add the olives and herbs, and cook 2 minutes more. Stir in the lemon juice and remove from the heat. Season with salt and pepper and let cool completely.

For the eggplant: Just prior to serving, make the salad. In a large serving bowl combine the lettuce, cucumbers, tomatoes, onion, feta, olive oil, lemon juice and herbs with the eggplant and croutons, and toss together. Season with salt and pepper.

Stuffed Grape Leaves

Makes about 50

Stephanie grew up in Phoenix, and once a year she would go to the pick-your-own Thompson grape field and pick leaves for her Auntie Violet, a first-generation Lebanese-American, to freeze for the entire year. Now we wait for the first tender leaves in the vineyard and pick them as we need them. Ground chicken or turkey also works for this recipe, as does the addition of chopped preserved lemon and chopped mint.

2 tablespoons olive oil
½ cup chopped onion
1 clove garlic, chopped
1 tablespoon chopped oregano
1 pound ground beef or lamb
½ cup uncooked white rice
⅔ cup water
½ teaspoon cinnamon
1 teaspoon salt
½ teaspoon pepper
50 young tender grape leaves
2 lemons, sliced

In a medium sauté pan over medium-high heat, heat the olive oil and sauté the onions until translucent, about 10 minutes. Stir in the garlic in the last 2 or 3 minutes, then add the oregano. Remove from the heat and let cool.

In a large bowl combine thoroughly the onions, ground meat, rice, ⅔ cup water, cinnamon, salt, and pepper.

Cut the stems from the grape leaves and lay flat with the rib side facing up and the base of the leaf at 6 o'clock. Mound 1 tablespoon of filling on the bottom third of each leaf. Fold the two bottom lobes of the leaf up over the filling, continuing to roll from the bottom, leaving a peephole of the filling in the middle at the base of the stem. Then fold in the sides, and lastly the top to cover the peephole, forming a cylinder.

In a large pot, layer the leaves seam side down. The pot should be no more than ⅔ full. Use another pot if necessary. Cover the grape leaves with one lemon's worth of slices. Place a plate that fits inside the saucepan over the top of the leaves to weight them down, then cover the leaves and plate with water.

Bring to a boil over high, reduce the heat, cover the pot with a lid and simmer for 40 minutes. Remove from the pot and serve with lemon slices and Lemon Yogurt Vinaigrette (page 98).

Toasted Pita Chips
with Hummus
Serves 6

Good pita chips and hummus can be bought at the store, but we like to make our own. The hummus recipe is a basic to which many flavors may be added, including chipotle chilies in adobo, sundried tomatoes, cooked beets, cooked pumpkin, roasted or raw jalapeños and dill, preserved lemon and sunflower seeds.

If you are cooking your own garbanzo beans, for an extra creamy consistency add a pinch of baking soda to the soaking water, then drain and cook the beans.

Pita Chips
3 pitas
3 tablespoons olive oil
1 clove garlic, minced
½ teaspoon salt
¼ teaspoon pepper

Hummus
1 (15-ounce) can of garbanzo beans, drained
¼ to ½ cup tahini
½ cup olive oil
2 cloves garlic, minced
Juice of 2 lemons
1 teaspoon salt

For the pita chips: Preheat the oven to 375°F.

Cut the pitas into 8 wedges and place in a mixing bowl. Drizzle on the olive oil, garlic, salt, and pepper, and toss to coat. Arrange in a single layer on a baking sheet and bake for 15 minutes, or until crispy and golden brown. Cool completely. These may be made ahead and stored in an airtight container.

For the hummus: Place the garbanzos, tahini, olive oil, garlic, lemon, and salt in an 11-cup food processor. Process until completely smooth. Adjust the seasonings to taste. This will keep 3 to 4 days in the fridge.

Freekeh
with Lemon and Herbs

Serves 6

Freekeh, also called farik, is young, green wheat, roasted and rubbed so the straw and chaff come off. Hailed as a "supergrain," it is low in gluten and has a nice, light smoky flavor.

1 cup freekeh
2 tablespoons extra-virgin olive oil
½ onion, chopped
1 clove garlic, minced
1¼ cups water or stock
1 tablespoon butter
2 teaspoons lemon juice
2 tablespoons chives, parsley, or dill
Salt and pepper

Soak the freekeh in water for 30 minutes, and drain.

Heat the olive oil in a medium saucepan over medium heat, and sauté the onion 5 minutes. Add the garlic to the onion and continue cooking until the onion is translucent, about 5 minutes more. Add the drained freekeh and 1¼ cups of water or stock, bring to a boil, cover, reduce heat to low, and cook for 15 minutes more. Don't peek. Let sit for 10 minutes then fluff with a fork and season with the butter, lemon, chives, and salt and pepper. May be served hot or at room temperature.

Quinoa
with Citrus Tahini

Serves 8

2 cups quinoa, soaked for at least 30 minutes
1 teaspoon salt
1 clove garlic, minced
¼ cup golden raisins, chopped
¼ cup tahini
4 tablespoons lemon juice
4 tablespoons olive oil
3 tablespoons water
½ cup chopped parsley
2 tablespoons minced chives
½ cup pistachios, toasted and chopped

Drain the quinoa and rinse with cold water. In a 2-quart saucepan bring 2½ cups of water to boil. Add the drained quinoa and salt, cover, reduce the heat, and cook for 15 minutes. Remove from the heat and fluff with a fork.

While the quinoa is cooking, mix the garlic, raisins, tahini, lemon juice, olive oil, and 3 tablespoons of water together in a small bowl and whisk until smooth. Stir the dressing into the quinoa with the parsley, chives, and pistachios. Season to taste.

Deviled Eggs with Anchovy

Makes 12

Banish the anchovy-naysayers! These eggs are absolutely addictive. I first had them years ago at a memorable picnic in the English countryside, where they were prepared simply with homemade mayonnaise and anchovies. We've embellished them with giardiniera relish and chives, but you can happily fall back to the simpler version. We like to use medium-size eggs for these.

Note: Giardiniera is an Italian condiment of spicy pickled vegetables that might include red and green peppers, jalapenos, celery, carrots, onions, and cauliflower. As a relish it is popular on sandwiches, hot dogs, sausages, pizza, and even as a stand-alone hors d'oeuvre.

6 medium eggs, hard-boiled and peeled
¼ cup Anchovy Aioli (page 54, omit the anchovy)
12 whole anchovy filets
2 teaspoons finely chopped, spicy Italian giardiniera
2 teaspoons chopped chives

Slice the eggs in half lengthwise and place on a serving platter. Top each half with ¼ teaspoon of the chopped giardiniera, a heaping teaspoon of aioli, an anchovy filet, and a sprinkle of chives.

Pistachio Almond Butter Cake

Makes a 9-inch square cake

Moist and deeply flavorful, there is more to this divine cake than its low key title lets on. To make gluten-free, substitute almond meal for flour. It's great.

Cake
½ cup almonds
½ cup pistachios
¾ cup all-purpose flour
1 teaspoon baking powder
¾ teaspoon salt
¾ cup butter, room temperature, plus more for the pan
1 cup sugar, plus more for the pan
Zest from 1 lemon
½ vanilla bean, split and scraped (optional)
2 eggs

Topping
Crush together in a mortar and pestle:
   2 tablespoons turbinado sugar
   2 tablespoons pistachios
   ¼ teaspoon salt

To make the cake: Preheat the oven to 350°F.
   Butter and sugar a 9-inch, parchment paper–lined pan.
   In a food processor, grind the almonds and pistachios to a fine meal. Add the flour, baking powder, and salt, and whir for 5 seconds. In a separate bowl and using an electric mixer, cream the butter and sugar with the lemon zest and vanilla bean scrapings until light and fluffy, about 4 minutes. Add the dry nut mixture alternately with the eggs in thirds, beginning and ending with the nut mixture. Spread into the pan and cover with the sugar and nut topping. Bake for 30 to 40 minutes until golden brown and a tester inserted in the middle comes out dry. Cool before cutting into squares to serve.

Menu

Caviar and Crisps

Chilled Corn Soup
with Crabmeat

Roasted Salmon
with Miso Mushroom Butter

New Potatoes
with Green Beans

Lemon Posset

Sbrisolona Cookies

Chapter 10
Small, Simple, Elegant

There is something so nice about a small dinner at home. To celebrate quietly or to mark a milestone—a low-key birthday, a deadline met, an obstacle overcome. At a table of four to six, you are truly able to be with one another without the pressure of a ready-clever riposte or the tedium of small talk that may creep into larger assemblies. Smaller groups also afford the luxury of a single conversation in which all participate, but try as I do to enforce this discipline, I often fail. Go with the flow—to a point anyway.

Practically speaking, dinners for small groups are more easily managed than those for a throng, especially for the novice host. With smaller groups you can hone your skills of preparation and timing. Dinner parties, like life, are all about timing. Learning by doing is the only way to integrate into your soirée-giving psyche how much time it really takes to set the table, do the flowers, organize the bar, light the candles, and so on. Carving out bits of time in the days ahead to accomplish some of these tasks saves you doing it all the day of. In the kitchen, too, there is a knack for when to cook what, how long to reheat, and what needs attention *à la minute*. Do accept your guests' offers of help, and, better still, think in advance what you can have them do when they ask.

Intimate gatherings are also the perfect time for a little splurge, to bring out the caviar, the foie gras, or the truffle something. Respect your budget of course, but may I say also that entertaining one's friends is not the time to "strike a blow for the economy," as Elsa Maxwell once put it. No one thrills to a bargain more than I, but when it comes to your near and dear, have the best you can afford. After that, a well-planned menu that allows you as host to relax, allows your guests to relax as well, and moreover to feel indulged, privileged, and pampered.

Caviar on potato chips is one of those high-low combinations I love. And for my money, potato chips beat the pants off blinis any day. The Miso

Mushroom Butter is an interesting and gorgeous accompaniment to the salmon. This dish is the only part of the dinner that requires a bit of last-minute attention. Roasting the potatoes and green beans imparts deeper, earthier flavor than boiling them, and they play well with the miso-mushroom salmon. The Lemon Posset, prepared in advance, is a creamy and light counterpoint to the crunchy, semi-sweet Sbrisolona cookies, and the perfect finish.

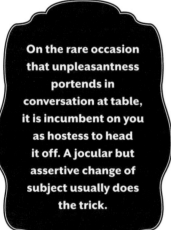

On the rare occasion that unpleasantness portends in conversation at table, it is incumbent on you as hostess to head it off. A jocular but assertive change of subject usually does the trick.

Caviar and Crisps

Simple, exquisite, extravagant, worth it. "Crisps" are what the English (and we) call potato chips because it sounds more elegant. There is no one way to do this, but we find it is prettier and less messy to prepare as a canape and to serve or pass on a plate. Choose a sturdy potato chip, like Ruffles, or one of those "gourmet" varieties. You don't want them tumbling to the carpet. Bad enough for the rug, but tragic for the caviar.

Buy the best caviar you feel like paying for; there are numerous sources for caviar online, and larger cities of course have specialty markets that will usually let you taste. But as it is such a special item I prefer a trusted source. We've always been pleased with Caviar Select (www.caviarselect.com) and Petrossian (petrossian.com). Both have wide selections and excellent customer service.

Potato Chips
Caviar
Sour cream or crème fraîche
Chopped chives

On each chip, place about half a teaspoon of caviar and a quarter teaspoon of sour cream or crème fraiche and a sprinkle of chives on top.

Chilled Corn Soup
with Crabmeat
Serves 4

The ginger and sage give this corn soup a brightness that other corn soups seem to lack, bless their hearts. The soup may also be served hot, but be sure to cool it before blending to avoid a messy and possibly dangerous eruption.

Soup

4 ears fresh corn, shucked and kernels cut away

4 cups corn stock (directions below), or chicken stock

3 tablespoons olive oil or butter

½ cup diced onion

1 clove garlic, minced

½ teaspoon minced fresh ginger

1 sprig of sage

Salt and pepper

Crabmeat

Lightly combine and refrigerate until ready to use:

¾ cup jumbo lump crabmeat

¼ cup chopped celery

2 tablespoons Basic Homemade Mayonnaise (page 42)

1 tablespoon chopped chives

1 tablespoon lemon juice

½ teaspoon salt

¼ teaspoon pepper

For the soup: To make a corn stock, break the shucked cobs in half and put into a stock pot. Cover the cobs with water (about 6 cups) and bring to a boil. Reduce the heat and simmer one hour. Strain the stock and discard the cobs. You should have 4 cups of corn stock.

In a medium pot over medium-high heat, heat the olive oil or butter. Add the onions, and sauté until soft, for 3 to 5 minutes, then add the garlic, ginger, and sage, and sauté another 2 minutes or so. Add the stock and bring to a simmer. Add the corn and return to a boil, season with salt and pepper, and remove from the heat. Cool to room temperature (see head note!) then purée in a blender. Transfer mixture to a heat-proof glass pitcher and refrigerate for 3 hours or until completely chilled.

Season with salt and pepper to taste. Divide the crabmeat into 4 bowls and ladle the soup around the crabmeat.

Roasted Salmon
with Miso Mushroom Butter
Serves 4

This is great on a buffet because it is good at room temperature. The bonus of fried onion rings is optional but they sure are good. See the note for cooking fish on page 79. This is one of those recipes that is good to read all the way through before beginning.

Miso Mushroom Butter is also excellent on beef or stirred into quinoa, farro, or any nutty grain. Freezes well for up to 3 months tightly wrapped in plastic.

Miso mushroom butter

3 tablespoons olive oil

1 pound mushrooms

1 shallot, minced

1 clove garlic, minced

1 teaspoon salt

½ teaspoon pepper

1 lemon, juiced

½ cup butter, room temperature

½ cup miso paste

3 tablespoons minced parsley

Onion rings

1 red onion, peeled and very thinly sliced (for best results, use a mandoline; ours is a "Little Beni" Benriner Mandolin)

½ cup buttermilk

1 cup all-purpose flour

1 teaspoon salt

¼ teaspoon pepper

¼ teaspoon cayenne pepper

¼ teaspoon paprika

2 cups vegetable oil, or more for a countertop fryer

Salmon

4 (6-ounce) boneless salmon filets, about ¾-inch thick

Salt and pepper

3 tablespoons olive oil

2 tablespoons butter

(Continued on page 112)

For the miso mushroom butter: Heat the olive oil in a 12-inch sauté pan over high heat. Add the mushrooms and sear, shaking and stirring for 2 minutes. Add the shallot, garlic, salt, and pepper and cook for 1 minute more. Add the lemon juice, and set aside to cool. Once cooled, place in a food processor with the butter and miso and process for 1 minute or until the mushrooms are thoroughly chopped into the butter and miso. Pulse in the parsley. Keep at room temperature until ready to use.

For the onion rings: Cover the sliced onions with buttermilk and refrigerate for at least 1 hour. In a shallow container, mix together the flour, salt, pepper, cayenne pepper, and paprika. Heat the oil in a 2-quart saucepan or other fryer to 350°F. Drain the onions and discard the buttermilk. Working in batches, dredge the onions in the flour and shake off the excess, carefully place into the hot oil and stir gently as they fry to a golden brown. Drain on paper towels and season with salt and pepper. These can be made several hours ahead and re-warmed briefly in the oven before serving.

For the salmon: Preheat the oven to 400°F.

Season the salmon on both sides with salt and pepper. Heat a 12-inch sauté pan over high heat. Add the olive oil and slide the salmon filets into the pan. Add the butter and reduce the heat to medium-high. For a ¾-inch thickness, cooked to medium, cook 2 minutes on the first side and 3 minutes on the second side, basting with the pan butter. If you are unsure about doneness, cut into one piece to check. Don't overcook it. Pop the salmon into the preheated oven for 2 or 3 minutes if you want more cooking time without browning.

To serve: Top each piece of salmon with 3 tablespoons of the miso mushroom butter and place in the oven for 2 minutes. Arrange filets on a warmed platter and top with the onion rings.

New Potatoes with Green Beans
Serves 4

Try to find the tiny new potatoes, or baby red potatoes. Halve or quarter them if they are larger than you like.

1 pound small new potatoes, washed but not peeled
2 tablespoons olive oil
1 teaspoon salt
¼ teaspoon pepper
1 pound green beans, ends trimmed
¼ cup chopped dill

Preheat the oven to 450°F.

Toss the potatoes with the olive oil, salt, and pepper in a large bowl. Place in a single layer on a baking sheet and bake for 10 minutes. Add the green beans to the pan, stir around, and bake for an additional 20 minutes, or until the potatoes and beans are tender. Remove from the oven, toss with the dill, and adjust the seasoning.

A Southern girl needs a mantelpiece to do up, but be careful what you ask for. We added these atop the limestone surrounds for both fireplaces in the great room. At 13 and 17 feet respectively, decorating them is like being on the altar guild for the Temple of Dendur. Protea and eucalyptus work well together in arrangements, and both dry nicely. Here combined with oak branches and trumpet vine, which do not dry nicely, alas. The painting is by friend Hunt Slonem.

Lemon Posset

Serves 8

Simple and sublime, Lemon Posset is an old-fashioned—ancient, in fact—dessert that purportedly dates to Roman times. For best results with this recipe, use heavy cream that is pasteurized as opposed ultra-pasteurized—see side note. This recipe is inspired by one from Cook's magazine. Measure the reduced cream to make sure you have 2 cups exactly. We use my grandmother's Limoges pots de crème, but demitasse cups or any small ramekins will do.

2 cups heavy cream
⅓ cup sugar
6 tablespoons lemon juice
Grated zest of 1 lemon
Pinch of salt
Whipped cream and berries for serving, if desired

In a saucepan over medium high heat, bring the cream and sugar to a boil. Reduce the heat to medium-low and simmer about 20 minutes or until the liquid is reduced to 2 cups. Stir in the lemon juice, zest, and a pinch of salt. Pour into pots de crème, demitasses, or ramekins, and chill. Serve with a dollop of whipped cream, fresh berries, and a cookie.

The Crop of the Cream

Pasteurized cream has a fresher taste and whips better into stiff peaks. It also separates more easily into curds. Ultra-pasteurized cream has been heated to a higher temperature to obliterate all bacteria and has a longer shelf life than pasteurized. It has more of a "cooked" taste and doesn't separate as easily or whip as well as pasteurized.

Sbrisolona Cookies

Makes a 9 x 13-inch pan

Dunk this Italian cookie in sweet wine for dessert or serve it with ice cream or sorbet. Easy to make, with a gorgeous texture and just enough sweetness. Sbrisolona cookies freeze beautifully and make a nice hostess gift.

1 cup flour
½ cup cornmeal
¾ cup slivered almonds
½ cup crushed or chopped almonds
½ cup whole almonds
Scant ½ cup sugar
½ teaspoon salt plus more for sprinkling on the baked cookies
7 tablespoons cold butter, cubed
Zest of one lemon
1 egg
Powdered sugar for dusting

Preheat oven to 350°F.

Line a 9 x 13-inch baking pan with parchment paper.

Mix together the flour, cornmeal, all the almonds, sugar, and salt. Cut in butter and lemon zest using a fork or two knives, as you would for pie dough. Lightly stir in the egg and then knead together with your fingertips. Don't over-knead; the dough should be crumbly and shaggy. Pat loosely onto the prepared pan and bake for 30 to 35 minutes, until golden brown. Sprinkle heavily with powdered sugar and lightly with salt. Allow to cool and break into pieces.

Menu

~~~

Endive, Parsley, Walnuts,
and Blue Cheese

Pork Valentine

Roasted Broccolini

Potato and Celery Root Puree

Deep, Dark Chocolate Mystery

Chapter 11
Sweethearts' Dinner

I don't mean to have a Valentine's Dinner every year, it just seems to happen. What is a lovelier theme than love? Chocolate, possibly, and there you go: Valentine's Day. It doesn't have to be on the actual day of course, but somewhere in the vicinity is convenient, if you are shopping for table decorations, favors, and such. There are times when decorative clichés are just fine and this is one of them. Like a really good recipe, some things don't need to be messed with. Find an object or idea that strikes your fancy and leave it at that or build around it. Perhaps tie it in to an activity or assignment for your guests.

One year I asked guests to write or bring a poem to read aloud. The recitations were by turn hilarious, heart-felt, surprising in some cases, and sweet. It is fascinating what we learn from and about one another when we venture outside our comfort zones, which this was clearly doing for some. And without it I may never have learned of the World War II era English poet, writer, and bon vivant John Betjeman, nor heard his wholesomely scandalous "Subaltern's Love-song" so admirably recited, British accent and all, the final stanzas of which go:

> . . . Around us are Rovers and Austins afar,
> Above us the intimate roof of the car
> And here on my right is the girl of my choice
> With the tilt of her nose and the chime of her voice,
>
> And the scent of her wrap, and the words
> never said
> And the ominous, ominous dancing ahead.
> We sat in the car-park till twenty to one
> And now I'm engaged to Miss Joan Hunter Dunn.

I wouldn't have missed that for the world.

This year's dinner table was feminine, fun, and simpler than it looked. It is worth repeating that one or two flowers-objects-somethings repeated or used en masse can be very effective, as was the case with tulips and cherry blossoms plunked in clear wine bottles and randomly placed on the table. With lace-trimmed linens and a bit of ribbon, the effect was greater than the sum of its parts. I love it when that happens.

The menu began with its luscious chocolate ending in mind. A salad of endive and walnuts set up perfectly the richness of the stuffed pork tenderloin, and the Deep, Dark Chocolate Mystery Cake fulfilled its promise of ecstasy—mysteriously, of course.

Endive, Parsley, Walnuts, and Blue Cheese

Serves 6 to 8

Yes, do freeze the walnuts. It adds an unexpected textural and temperature element. Think of the parsley not as an accent herb here but part of the base of the salad. Pull the big leaves and fronds off of the tough stems.

Freezing walnuts in an endive salad is a tidbit we picked up in one of our favorite old cookbooks called The Private Collection *from the Junior League of Palo Alto. The walnuts seem to become creamier and the chill seeps into the endive, keeping it crisp and fresh tasting. So cool.*

4 heads Belgian endive
2 cups parsley leaves and fronds, with tough stems
    removed
5 tablespoons olive oil, divided
2 tablespoons lemon juice, divided
1 tablespoon balsamic vinegar
1 teaspoon Dijon mustard
1 clove garlic, minced
1 teaspoon salt
½ teaspoon pepper
2 tablespoons thinly sliced red onion
1 cup chopped walnuts, lightly toasted then frozen
½ cup crumbled blue cheese

Trim the ends from the endive and separate into individual leaves. Combine endive and parsley in a bowl and refrigerate until ready to use. Whisk together 4 tablespoons olive oil, 1 tablespoon lemon juice, vinegar, mustard, garlic, salt, and pepper. Just before serving, toss the endive and parsley with the red onion, 1 tablespoon of olive oil, 1 tablespoon of lemon juice, the frozen walnuts, blue cheese, salt, and pepper. Mound on individual plates or a large serving dish and drizzle with the dressing.

Roasted Broccolini

Serves 6

A quickly prepared, bright, and slightly bitter accompaniment for rich meat dishes, but good with everything.

1 lemon
2 pounds broccolini
2 tablespoon olive oil
2 cloves garlic, minced
1 teaspoon salt
¼ teaspoon pepper

Preheat the oven to 425°F.

Grate the zest of the lemon and then cut the lemon in half and set aside. Trim away the tough ends from the broccolini and chop into 1-inch pieces or thin, lengthwise slices. Toss with the olive oil, garlic, lemon zest, salt, and pepper. Lay in a single layer on a sheet pan lined with parchment paper and roast for 12 to 15 minutes or until the broccolini is tender. Remove from the oven and squeeze the lemon all over.

> ### Seeing Red . . .
> ### Flowers, that is.
> It is annoying that flower shops put up the prices of their roses around Valentine's Day, but that's the free market at work. One suggestion for beating it is to start amaryllis bulbs in December and hope for the best by February 14. Amaryllis plants are gorgeous on their own and showy in arrangements. Plenty of other flowers come in reds and pinks, too. My favorite peonies are sometimes available from wholesalers, and tulips, ranunculus, anemones, and carnations (yes!) are just a few.

Pork Valentine

Serves 4 to 6

This is Stephanie's take on the traditional Italian porchetta, consisting of a garlic- and herb-seasoned suckling pig, stuffed with bits of liver and meat and roasted in a wood oven. Steph's version has all the traditional elements with half the hassle. Absolutely sublime. It deserves to be named for the chef.

Note: A pork tenderloin usually weighs between ¾ and 1½ pounds, with a serving size between 3 and 4 ounces. They often come two to a package.

8 ounces sliced bacon
4 ounces pork sausage, such as bratwurst, removed
    from the casing
1 tablespoon chopped fresh herbs such as marjoram,
    rosemary, thyme, or oregano
1 whole pork tenderloin, silver-skin removed

Sauce
1 cup chicken stock
3 tablespoons Dijon mustard
3 tablespoons lemon juice
1 shallot, minced
1 clove garlic, minced
½ teaspoon salt
¼ teaspoon pepper

Preheat the oven to 425°F.

Lay the bacon slices out on a sheet of plastic wrap, overlapping slightly, to form a rectangle slightly larger than the length and circumference of the tenderloin. Place another sheet of plastic wrap on top and use the smooth side of a meat mallet to pound into a thin, even layer. Spread with the raw sausage or bratwurst and the chopped herbs. Place the tenderloin lengthwise an inch inside along the edge and roll firmly. Roast on a rack inside a roasting pan for about 25 minutes or to an internal temperature of 135°F. Remove from the oven, tent with foil, and let the meat rest for 10 minutes before slicing.

For the sauce: Deglaze the roasting pan with the chicken stock and stir up any brown bits. Pour into a small saucepan and whisk in the Dijon, lemon, olive oil, shallot, and garlic, and season with the salt and pepper.

Potato and Celery Root Puree

Serves 6

Celery root is among the homeliest of vegetables, but it tastes better than it looks. Easier to peel with a paring knife rather than with a peeler.

1½ pounds Idaho potatoes (about 3 large potatoes),
    peeled and cut into 1-inch chunks
½ pound celery root (about 1 large bulb), peeled and
    cut into 1-inch chunks
½ cup cream
¼ cup unsalted butter
Salt and pepper

Place the potato and celery root into an 8-quart saucepan and cover with water. Bring to a boil, add a generous pinch of salt, and reduce the heat to simmer for 15 minutes, or until the potatoes and celery root are fork tender. Drain, reserving a ¼ cup of the cooking liquid to set aside. Return vegetables to the pan with the cream and butter and mash or put through a food mill. If needed, soften with a bit of the reserved cooking liquid (or stock, cream, or hot water). Salt and pepper to taste.

Deep, Dark Chocolate Mystery

Serves 10 or more

The blend of licorice and chocolate is the deep and delicious mystery in this simplest and richest cake ever. Steph calls it her secret weapon and insists on the best quality chocolate, such as Vahlrona. Black sambuca is more syrupy than its white counterpart, with a more intense anise flavor. You may substitute orange or coffee liqueur for the sambuca, and the cake can be made gluten-free by replacing the small amount of flour with an equal amount of almond flour.

Note: If you don't have a springform pan, bake in a 10-inch cake pan and allow to cool for 10 minutes before removing. To remove, run a knife around the edge, place a plate over the pan, and invert the cake onto the plate. Place another plate on top of the cake and invert again to be right side up, and allow to cool completely.

11 ounces bittersweet chocolate, chopped
6 ounces unsalted butter
6 eggs, separated into whites and yolks
¾ cup light brown sugar
5 tablespoons flour, sifted
¼ cup black Sambuca (or other) liqueur
1 teaspoon vanilla extract
½ teaspoon salt
Whipped cream, for serving

Line the bottom of a 10-inch round springform pan with parchment, then butter and sugar the sides.

Preheat the oven to 350°F.

Melt the chocolate and butter together in a double boiler, and set aside to cool.

Beat the yolks with the sugar in a standing mixer until light in texture and color, about 5 minutes. Fold in the chocolate mixture, then gently fold in the flour. Add the Sambuca and the vanilla. Separately, beat the egg whites and salt together just until stiff peaks form and fold ⅓ of the whites into the chocolate mixture to lighten, and then gently fold in the remaining whites. Pour into the prepared pan, spreading evenly. Bake for 25 to 30 minutes. Remove from the oven, cool for 10 minutes on a rack, and then remove the sides of the pan to cool completely. Serve with whipped cream to which you've added a bit of liqueur and a little sugar.

Menu

~~~~~~~~

BLT Bites

Cauliflower Soup Demitasses

Herb and Garlic Roasted Veal

Soubise

Braised Endive

Roasted Asparagus

Ginger Sticky Toffee Pudding

Chapter 12
Club El Rancho

When you think of a chic and glamorous party setting, "Quonset hut horse barn" may not immediately spring to mind. But that's what we had and we went with it. Though it took a little convincing.

This Friday night party was second in the three-night celebration that was our wedding weekend, and we wanted each night to be different. The previous night's rollicking Western-themed fiesta hosted by Valley friends at their family ranch was a fitting bow to our rural Valley community and a joshing nod to my husband's cowboy-cattle-trading-Sioux-City-Chicago roots. The next night, as nearly half the guests and yours truly hailed from Back East, we channeled Café Society and Manhattan's fashionable old nightclub El Morocco . . . in a horse barn, in case you forgot. "Right," retorted my beloved betrothed. "Watch her," quipped I, knowing that to underestimate the talents of friend, floral and event designer Mindy Rice was utter foolishness.

Klieg lights beamed greetings to guests at the end of a winding road, where velvet ropes and red carpet marked the entrance. A stunning Deco-style mirrored bar made a grand statement inside, beyond which a zebra-painted dance floor gleamed and white leather(ish) banquettes beckoned beneath swaying palms. That, and enough gray polyester to cover the earth, and voila: a Cedric Gibbons sound stage. A neon sign above the bandstand proclaimed Club El Rancho, which was ridiculous but a hoot. Hoots are good because they are unexpected, and nothing delights your guests more.

If anything could have upstaged the décor, it would have been Chef Stephanie's meal. She shone this night like the star that she is, and the meal was perfection. Our menu here is modified from that night's, but it is no less transcendent, from the first course of creamy cauliflower soup, to the succulent veal roast, to a ginger sticky toffee pudding to make the angels sing.

BLT Bites

Makes 24

This is a great passed hors d'oeuvre and equally nice on a buffet.

¼ cup chopped red onion
1 tablespoon red wine vinegar
1 tablespoon water
½ teaspoon salt, divided
3 little gem lettuces, or 3 romaine hearts
3 hard boiled eggs, chopped
3 slices bacon, cooked and chopped
½ cup blue cheese crumbles
2 tablespoons chopped chives
½ cup Buttermilk Dressing (page 143)
Pepper

In a small bowl, combine the onion with the red wine vinegar, a tablespoon of water, and ¼ teaspoon salt, and set aside.

Trim the bottom from the lettuce and discard the tough outer leaves. Reserve 24 small individual leaves and save the rest of for another use. Sprinkle the leaves evenly with the chopped egg, bacon, blue cheese, and chives, then drizzle each with the buttermilk dressing. Strain the red onions and sprinkle those on top. Finish with a grind of black pepper over all.

Cauliflower Soup Demitasses

Makes 5 cups

This is the best cauliflower soup ever in the history of the universe. We also like to pass it as an hors d'oeuvre or stand-up first course in demitasses. It may also be served conventionally in bowls, of course. Garnish with roasted cauliflower florets and croutons, if desired. Also delicious cold.

2 tablespoons olive oil
½ cup chopped onion
1 clove garlic, chopped
⅛ teaspoon cumin seed
⅛ teaspoon coriander seed
⅛ teaspoon anise seed
1 (1-inch) shard of a cinnamon stick
1 pinch red pepper flakes
6 cups cauliflower florets
4 cups chicken stock
½ cup milk, whole or low fat
Salt and pepper
Roasted Cauliflower Florets and Croutons, if desired
     (recipe follows)

In a large stock pot over medium heat, add the olive oil and sauté the onion until soft, 10 to 15 minutes. In the last few minutes add the garlic, cumin, coriander, anise, cinnamon, and red pepper flakes. Add the cauliflower and stock and bring to a boil, then reduce the heat and stir in the milk. Simmer for 15 minutes, adding salt and pepper to taste. Cool the soup to room temperature before puréeing in a blender or food processor. For a more velvety texture, strain through a fine mesh strainer. Reheat gently, and garnish if desired.

Roasted Cauliflower Florets and Croutons
Optional but very good.

½–¾ cup cauliflower florets, chopped into ½-inch pieces
Olive oil
¾–1 cup of ¼-inch stale bread cubes
Salt and pepper

Heat oven to 425°F. Toss the chopped cauliflower with a tablespoon or two of olive oil and roast for 8 minutes, until well browned, shaking the pan to prevent burning. Heat a tablespoon or two of olive oil in a pan over medium-high heat, and fry the bread cubes, stirring until crisp. Season the cauliflower and croutons with salt and pepper, and sprinkle on the soup.

With such an elaborate overall scheme, "Club El Rancho" kept the flowers simple and elegant: Yves Piaget roses, pink orchids, and palms. Overleaf: Oh ye of little faith. If you ever doubted that a decorating challenge could be met with 72,000 yards of gray polyester, now you know. Et voilà: how a horse barn becomes a nightclub. And lest there be any doubt, we had a sign made to remind us. Channeling the old El Morocco, we had a gleaming zebra-patterned dance floor and zebra print pillows on the dining banquettes.

Herb and Garlic Roasted Veal

Serves 6 to 8

The flavorful veal shoulder is at its best braised or roasted long and slowly as we do here. The anchovy dissolves completely and you won't know it's there but for the traces of its briny deliciousness.

1 (3-pound) veal shoulder roast, tied

2 teaspoons salt

½ teaspoon pepper

2 tablespoons olive oil

1 onion, sliced

1 anchovy filet, optional

1 clove garlic, minced

1 Roma tomato, chopped

1 tablespoon tomato paste

1 cup red wine

3 sprigs fresh thyme

Preheat a 4-quart Dutch oven over high heat. Season the veal roast with the salt and pepper. Add the olive oil to the pan and sear the veal on all sides, remove from the pan and set aside. Preheat the oven to 300°F. Add the onions and anchovy to the pan, reduce the heat to medium-low, cook, stirring occasionally, for about 15 minutes, until the onions are browned and the anchovy dissolved. In the last few minutes, add the garlic. Add the tomato and tomato paste, cooking 2 minutes more. Add the wine and thyme, and bring to a simmer.

Add the veal back to the pot, cover, and place in the 300°F oven for 1½ to 2 hours, turning the roast over halfway through. Cook to an internal temperature of 160°F. Remove from the oven and allow to rest for 30 minutes before slicing. Remove the thyme sprigs and pour the pan juices in into a small pan to keep warm. Season the pan juices to taste and serve with the sliced meat.

Soubise

Serves 8

This creamy, cheesy onion–rice dish is a divine accompaniment to roasted meats, serving as both a side dish and a kind of sauce. I credit the artful host, chef, Southerner, Francophile, and friend Alex Hitz with introducing me to this French classic at a dinner in his gorgeous former Beverly Hills home. This is Stephanie's rendition, and she cautions to read it through before beginning so you allow ample time.

4 tablespoons butter
2½–3 pounds onions, half diced and half thinly sliced
2 sprigs thyme
½ cup risotto rice, such as Arborio or carnaroli
Salt and pepper to taste
½ cup grated Gruyere cheese
¼ cup grated Parmesan cheese
⅔ cup heavy cream
1 tablespoon lemon juice
2 tablespoons chopped parsley

Preheat oven to 300°F.

Melt the butter in a 4-quart Dutch oven over medium heat. Add the onions and thyme and cook slowly for 15 to 20 minutes until the onions are translucent, stirring often and lowering the heat if the onions start to brown.

As the onions cook, in a separate pot bring 2 cups of water to a boil and add the rice. Cook for 6 minutes and drain. Add the rice to the cooked onions with the salt and pepper and stir to combine. Cover the Dutch oven and place it in the oven and cook for 35 minutes. Don't peek—the rice needs to steam and cook. Remove from the oven and let it sit, covered, 30 minutes more. Before serving, return the pot to the stovetop on medium-low heat and add the cheeses, cream, and lemon juice, stirring until thoroughly hot. Sprinkle with the parsley to finish.

Braised Endive

Serves 4 to 8

Braised Endive is a classic dish that is especially good with roasted meats or chicken. I don't know why we don't see it more. It is also good by itself with a side of mashed potatoes. Look for endive that are white and yellow. The more green they are, the more bitter. Endive is also delicious raw and sliced into any salad green mix.

2 tablespoons olive oil
4 heads endive, trimmed and cut in half, lengthwise
2 tablespoons butter
1 shallot, minced
1 clove garlic, minced
½ teaspoon sugar
¾ teaspoon salt
¼ teaspoon pepper
1 tablespoon lemon juice
½ cup chicken stock or water
2 sprigs thyme

Heat a 12-inch sauté pan over medium-high heat. Add the olive oil, and when it is shimmering add the endives cut side down in a single layer. Add the butter and brown the endive about 2 minutes, then turn and brown the other side. Stir in the shallot and garlic, and season with the sugar, salt, and pepper. Add the lemon juice, stock or water, and thyme, shaking the pan to "stir" the endive. Cover, reduce the heat to low, and cook for 12 to 15 minutes or until the endives are tender all the way through.

Roasted Asparagus

Serves 6

For best results when roasting, choose asparagus that is at least as thick as a little finger. The very thin spears shrivel under high heat.

2 pounds asparagus
1 tablespoon olive oil
1 clove garlic, minced
1 teaspoon salt
¼ teaspoon pepper
Half a lemon

Preheat the oven to 425°F.

Trim the tough ends from the asparagus and toss with the olive oil, garlic, salt, and pepper. Lay in a single layer on a parchment paper-lined baking sheet and roast for 10 to 12 minutes or until the asparagus is tender when pierced with a fork. Give a squeeze of lemon before serving.

Ginger Sticky Toffee Pudding

Makes 9 servings or 1 (9-inch) square pan

Really a moist, rich cake, our Ginger Sticky Toffee Pudding is a twist on a beloved classic. The addition of crystallized ginger in truth was at first an accident, but a happy one, and now we won't have it any other way. But if you don't have ginger, proceed without, it is still delicious.

For the toffee sauce
Makes 2¼ cups

1½ cups light brown sugar
2 cups cream
2 tablespoons butter
¾ teaspoon salt
1 teaspoon vanilla extract

For the cake
Butter and flour, for the pan
½ cup chopped walnuts
4 tablespoons chopped crystallized ginger, divided
8 ounces Medjool dates, pitted and chopped
1 teaspoon baking soda
4 tablespoons butter
¾ cup brown sugar
2 whole eggs
1 cup flour
1 teaspoon baking powder
½ teaspoon ground ginger
½ teaspoon salt

For the toffee sauce: In a 2-quart saucepan stir together the brown sugar, cream, butter, and salt. Bring to a boil, reduce the heat, and simmer for 5 minutes. Remove from the heat and stir in the vanilla.

For the cake: Preheat the oven to 325°F.

Butter and flour the sides of a 9-inch square cake pan and line the bottom with parchment paper. Scatter the walnuts and 2 tablespoons of the crystalized ginger over the bottom and pour ¾ cup of toffee sauce over them.

Place the dates, remaining ginger, and baking soda in a heatproof bowl, pour in 1 cup of boiling water, stir, and let sit.

In a stand mixer cream the butter and sugar together until light and fluffy, about 4 minutes. Add the eggs, beating after each addition. In a small bowl sift together the flour, baking powder, ginger, and salt. Add the flour mixture to the butter and stir just until blended. Add the dates with the liquid and mix together on low speed, just until incorporated. Scrape into the prepared pan and bake for 40 to 45 minutes or until a toothpick inserted in the center comes out clean.

Remove the cake from the oven and cool for 10 minutes, then invert onto an oven-proof serving plate or sheet pan and pour 1½ cups of the remaining sauce over the cake, allowing it to soak in. To serve, re-heat the sauced cake under the broiler for 1 to 2 minutes, until it is hot and bubbly, careful not to scorch the sugar.

Serve with vanilla ice cream or whipped cream and have the extra warm sauce nearby.

Variation: Poached pears or apples can be added to the bottom of the pan, or even sliced poached kumquats.

Menu

Seasoned Persian Cucumbers

Mushroom and Taleggio Toast

Escarole and Radicchio Salad
with Bacon and Herbs

Seared Steak La Zaca

Potatoes au Gratin

Sautéed Spinach

Pavlova
with Chestnut Purée
and Toasted Almonds

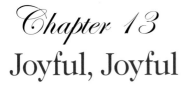

Chapter 13
Joyful, Joyful

Reader, I married him.

But like Jane Eyre in Charlotte Brontë's novel, it was not a foregone conclusion. Both Jane's Mr. Rochester and my Mr. Dittmer were already married—to other people. Tom was in the midst of divorce when we met in late 2008, and I myself had just cancelled a wedding, as chronicled in my previous *The Bee Cottage Story: How I Made a Muddle of Things and Decorated My Way Back to Happiness*. Understandably at the time, neither of us were thinking about knot-tying again, but after a four-year courtship, we were.

Well, you can put your life on hold or you can get on with it. We picked a date and planned a hoopla, wedding or no. I figured the bride and groom from AARP could marry as happily at the Santa Barbara County Courthouse as anywhere, but celebrating it (sooner or later) called for a more festive venue. We had sent a save-the-date but held the invitations until the last minute, pending the, um, appropriate wording.

As with the rehearsal dinner the night before, we were guided by Mindy Rice and event planner Lisa Vorce for design and logistics. The wedding, now proceeding after all (!), would be in the olive grove and the reception by the pond. Guests had the option of walking the path through lavender and prairie grass meadow, or shuttling by our ragtag fleet of

golf cart–like utility vehicles, terribly glamorous. The outdoor setting lent itself to less formality than the fancy pants night before. Gentlemen wore suits and the ladies wore long or short dresses. All were advised of cool evening temperatures and gravelly, sandy footing. Nevertheless, we provided a basket of inexpensive ivory shawls that guests were free to take, and thoughtful, generous friend donated rather chic, bronze colored flip-flops.

The décor was inspired by nature in all her autumn glory, from the oak plank tables and woven rush seating to the nubby brown linens in richly toned embroidery. The rustic elegance was understated and just right, but Mindy's flowers, restrained the night before, this night were swoon-worthy. Hydrangeas, roses, peonies, autumn fruits, amaryllis, amaranth, branches of fig, and boughs of bittersweet, with my Southern magnolia in there for good measure—a more artless expression of setting and season there could not have been. But I am a teeny bit biased.

Growing up in the South, we did not have seated dinners after weddings owing to the widespread sentiment that it interfered with the drinking, though one does not say such things these days. The seated business and toasts and what-all were for the night before, and the reception afterward was all about dancing and flitting about, activities inevitably impeded by the captivity of a seated dinner. So we kept to the old Southern way with a free-range reception.

As Chef Stephanie was a guest this night, the evening was catered by the incomparable Wolfgang Puck. He and his team delivered flawlessly with all manner of hors d'oeuvres and small dishes, and a bountiful raw bar was set up on the dock. I barely ate, but I danced, honey, as did we all, from the first song to the last. The music was out of control fantastic, and I declare as does His Grace that the music is The Thing. And I mean the kind of music that people can't keep still to. They just can't. That's what makes a great party like this. It just does.

Our menu here would satisfy the lustiest of appetites and fuel the body to dance all night, from a mushroom and taleggio hors d'oeuvre, to a tangy sauced steak, to a decadent chestnut and chocolate dream of dessert. It's a tremendous crowd-pleaser and a guaranteed rave-winner. Reader, you'll love it.

Seasoned Persian Cucumbers

Delicious as a light hors d'oeuvre and also lovely as a luncheon item. If you do not have Persian cucumbers, the regular kind will do, just peel and seed them before cutting lengthwise into spears. Persian cucumbers don't need peeling.

4 Persian cucumbers, ends trimmed and cut lengthwise
    into 6 spears each
2 tablespoons white wine vinegar
2 cloves garlic, sliced
¼ teaspoon red pepper flakes
1 teaspoon chopped fresh thyme, optional
½ teaspoon salt
½ teaspoon pepper
Juice from 1 lime
1 tablespoon chopped fresh dill

Toss the cucumber spears with the vinegar, garlic, red pepper flakes, thyme, salt, and pepper. Cover and refrigerate for one hour. Just before serving, toss with the lime juice and dill.

Escarole and Radicchio Salad
with Bacon and Herbs
Serves 6 to 8

A tasty and unusual salad, with the added earthy richness of truffled cheese. We use gouda, but any truffled cheese will do. Any mix of bitter greens is great in this salad: escarole, radicchio, treviso, frisée, or endive. Little gem and butter lettuces, or even a good old iceberg wedge would be delicious too.

Buttermilk Dressing
½ cup buttermilk

½ cup Basic Homemade Mayonnaise (page 42)

½ cup sour cream

2 tablespoons chopped parsley, or a mix of any herbs

2 teaspoons lemon juice

½ teaspoon onion powder

½ teaspoon garlic powder

½ teaspoon dried thyme

½ teaspoon salt

½ teaspoon pepper

In a 2-quart bowl, whisk together all ingredients. Will keep several days in the fridge.

Salad
3 heads escarole, tough outer green leaves removed, and yellow inner leaves chopped in small bite-size pieces

2 heads radicchio, outer leaves removed, cored and cut into bite-size wedges

¼ cup coarsely chopped tarragon leaves

½ cup coarsely chopped mint leaves

¾ cup chopped dill sprigs

½ cup chives, cut in ¾-inch lengths

1 tablespoon lemon juice

2 tablespoons olive oil

Salt and pepper

½ cup Buttermilk Dressing (recipe above)

½ cup cooked, chopped bacon, optional

½ cup grated, truffled cheese, gouda or other

To assemble: In a large mixing bowl, toss together the escarole and radicchio with the tarragon, mint, dill, chives, lemon, olive oil, salt, and pepper. Spoon 1 tablespoon each of buttermilk dressing onto the bottom of 6 or 8 salad plates. Divide the salad mixture between the plates and top with the bacon (if using) and grated cheese, and drizzle with the remaining dressing. Or toss all together in a large salad bowl and sprinkle the bacon and cheese on top.

Variations: A lemon and olive oil vinaigrette is equally good on this salad, in lieu of the Buttermilk Dressing. Adding a bit of fruit and nuts makes interesting combinations as well. Persimmons, pomegranate seeds, roasted beets, toasted walnuts, and feta or blue cheese would all be good. Not all at once, mind you, just two or so at a time.

Mushroom and Taleggio Toast

Makes 24 pieces

Taleggio is a pungent and soft cow's milk cheese from Northern Italy. It has a lovely melting quality and the flavor holds up well with the Portobello mushrooms. The mushrooms and filling can be prepared 2 days in advance.

Mushrooms

2 large Portobello mushrooms, stalks and underside ribs
    scraped out with a spoon

2 tablespoons olive oil

Salt and pepper

Filling

2 tablespoons olive oil

½ small onion, finely diced

1 celery stalk, trimmed and finely diced

½ cup finely chopped, oil packed sun-dried tomatoes

1 clove garlic, minced

½ cup grated Parmesan cheese

1 tablespoon chopped tarragon

2 tablespoons chopped basil, plus more for serving

Salt and pepper

3 ounces Taleggio cheese

Toast

1 baguette, cut into ⅛-inch slices

3 tablespoons olive oil

For the mushrooms: Preheat the oven to 350°F.

On a parchment paper–lined baking sheet, place the mushrooms stalk side up. Drizzle with olive oil and season with salt and pepper. Roast for 15 to 20 minutes, until the mushrooms are softened and cooked through. Slice each mushroom into ⅛-inch slices.

For the filling: In a 10-inch sauté pan, heat the olive oil, add the onion and celery, and cook on low heat for 8 to 10 minutes until the vegetables are soft but not brown. Add the sun-dried tomatoes and garlic and cook 3 more minutes. Remove from the heat and cool. Add the Parmesan, tarragon, and basil, and season with salt and pepper, keeping in mind that the Taleggio cheese is a bit salty.

For the toast: Preheat the oven to 400°. Brush the baguette slices with olive oil and bake for 2 or 3 minutes until the edges are lightly browned.

To serve: Heat the oven to broil.

Top each baguette with 2 slices of mushroom and a teaspoon of the sundried tomato filling. Top with a slice of Taleggio and broil for 1 minute, or until the cheese is melted and bubbly. Garnish with torn basil and serve.

Potatoes au Gratin

Serves 12

Au gratin potatoes are old fashioned but timeless and delicious. Great with any meat, or a hearty vegetarian dish on their own. Don't worry about the herbs; use what herbs you have or none. For the cheese, we use a mix of Gruyère and Parmesan, but any will do. If you do not need 12 servings, divide the recipe between 2 casseroles and freeze one for later.

Note: Recipes are famous for fibbing about how long it takes to caramelize onions. Only light caramelizing is called for here. Deep caramelizing takes half again as long. Patience, dear.

3 tablespoons olive oil

3 onions, thinly sliced

3 tablespoons butter, plus more for the pan

Juice of 1 lemon, about 4 tablespoons

4 tablespoons chopped fresh herbs, such as thyme, oregano, marjoram, or rosemary

Salt and pepper

3 pounds potatoes, peeled

3 cups cream

3 cups grated cheese

1½ tablespoons chopped chives

1½ tablespoons chopped parsley

Heat a 12-inch sauté pan over high heat. Add the olive oil and the onion, stir to coat the onion. Add the butter and reduce the heat to medium. Cook, stirring occasionally, until the onions are light brown, about 25 minutes. Stir in the lemon juice and herbs, and season with salt and pepper.

In a separate small pot, heat the cream to steaming, but do not boil.

Butter a 13 x 9-inch pan or casserole dish.

Preheat the oven to 375°F with a rack in lower third of the oven.

Slice the potatoes into ⅛-inch-thick rounds, and make 2 layers in the bottom of the buttered dish. Season with salt and pepper, and pour in 1 cup of hot cream.

Cover with a third of the onions and a third of the cheese over the top, and sprinkle with a third of the chives and parsley. Repeat 2 more layers and place on a sheet pan to catch drippings. Bake for 1 hour or until the potatoes are cooked through, fork tender, and golden brown. Cover with foil if the potatoes begin to brown too much.

Variation

Using the same ingredients and same quantities, this is a quicker "homestyle" version, and just as tasty.

Preheat the oven to 375°F.

In a pan large enough to hold all the onions and potatoes, caramelized the onions as above.

Slice the potatoes ¼-inch thick and add to the caramelized onions. Add the hot cream and season with salt and pepper. Cook and turn the onions and potatoes together for about 10 minutes. Put a third of the onion-potato mixture into the buttered casserole and layer with one third of the herbs and cheese, making three layers ending with the cheese. Bake for 50 to 60 minutes until the potatoes are completely cooked and golden brown.

Sauce Notes

A great steak stands alone, but for those who like sauces (and we do), the steak is tastier and juicier still. In addition to our Sauce La Zaca, try a vinaigrette of olive oil and lemon juice or balsamic vinegar. Adding sautéed mushrooms or onions with a splash of lemon juice or balsamic at the end is tasty, too.

Cast Iron

Cast iron is a brilliant cooking surface because it holds heat so well, but it does not preheat evenly. Let it preheat 10 minutes or so on the burner, rotating it occasionally. This is especially important in searing and cooking meat.

Seared Steak La Zaca

Serves 4 to 8

What makes this so delicious is the crust that forms by searing the beef in a hot iron skillet. Grilling works too, of course! We find that half of a large ribeye is enough for a serving, but you may have major carnivores on hand who will eat more, hence the range of serving portions from 4 to 8. Tenderloin and other cuts of beef may also be used.

4 ribeye steaks, each 1½-inches thick
Kosher salt, or other coarsely grained salt
Olive oil
Coarsely ground pepper
Sauce La Zaca (recipe follows)

Early in the day, dry the steaks with paper towels, sprinkle both sides with salt, and place on a rack over a plate or baking sheet in the refrigerator.

When ready to cook, preheat the oven to 500°F and place the oven baking rack in the lowest position. Preheat a 12-inch iron skillet over high heat until hot (see Side Note).

Rub both sides of the steaks with oil, sprinkle on more salt and liberally grind with pepper. Sear the steaks for 30 seconds per side. Place the pan with the steaks in the preheated oven and cook for 2 minutes per side for medium rare. Remove the steaks from the pan to a cutting board and let rest for a minute or 2 before slicing. Serve alongside the Sauce La Zaca.

Sauce La Zaca

Good on beef and chicken, this Sauce La Zaca is really a New Orleans–style barbeque sauce, with our California–Southern spin. The hot pepper addition gives an extra zing, but it is just as good without. The jalapeño is milder than the serrano.

1 tablespoon olive oil
½ jalapeño or serrano pepper, seeded and thinly sliced
1 shallot, chopped
2 cloves garlic, chopped
1 tablespoon lemon juice
¼ cup Worcestershire sauce
4 tablespoons butter

In a saucepan over medium heat, heat the olive oil and fry the sliced pepper for 1 minute. Add the shallots and garlic and stir 2 or 3 minutes more. Don't let the garlic burn. Add the lemon juice to deglaze the pan, then the Worcestershire sauce, and bring to a boil. Remove from the heat and whisk in the butter.

Sautéed Spinach

Serves 8

Simple. This would also work for kale, which you may want to sauté a minute or two longer.

3 tablespoons olive oil
1–2 tablespoons butter
1 clove garlic, sliced
1 shallot, sliced
Pinch of red chili flakes
Salt and pepper
2–3 bunches spinach (or kale), stemmed and washed

In a Dutch oven over medium-high heat, add the olive oil and butter. When the butter is melted, quickly sauté the garlic, shallot, and chili flakes, add salt and pepper, and gently stir in the spinach just until wilted. Taste and adjust the seasonings, and give another drizzle of olive oil.

Pavlova

with Chestnut Purée, Toasted Almonds, and Chocolate Sauce

Serves 8–10

The meringue-and-cream concoction also known as Pavlova is a beloved dessert in all its forms at Rancho La Zaca. Simple and easy to prepare, but most impressive. The chestnut puree and almonds can be made several days in advance. Pair it with the Chocolate Sauce recipe on page 66. This meringue recipe is from our New Zealander friend Susan Jaques.

Note: In summer, top meringues with fresh berries, sliced kiwi, and whipped cream.

Meringue

6 large egg whites, at room temperature
½ teaspoon salt
1½ cups sugar
1½ teaspoons vinegar (preferably white wine vinegar, but cider vinegar will do as well)
¾ teaspoon vanilla extract
2 tablespoons cornstarch

Chestnut Purée

2 cups chestnuts
½ cup sugar
1 cinnamon stick
1 cup water

Almonds

1 cup almonds
1 teaspoon water
3 tablespoons sugar
½ teaspoon cinnamon
¼ teaspoon salt

Whipped Cream

2 cups heavy cream
3 tablespoons sugar
1 teaspoon vanilla extract

> To make a perfect round meringue, use a cake pan to trace a circle onto a sheet of parchment paper. Turn the paper over (so the pencil marks don't fade onto the meringue) and adhere to pan with dabs of meringue. Spread meringue mixture onto the circle and bake.

For the meringue: Preheat oven to 350°F.

Beat the whites and salt on medium-high speed until they are just barely stiff. Start adding the sugar 1 tablespoon at a time and whip until very stiff and glossy. Change from the whisk to the paddle attachment, add the vinegar, vanilla, and cornstarch, and beat on high speed for 10 minutes, no less!

Onto a parchment-lined baking sheet, mound the meringue into a 10-inch circle, or 8 (3½-inch) circles. Place in the oven, immediately turn the temperature to 250°F. Bake 1½ hours for the large Pavlova, or 1 hour and 15 minutes for the small. Turn oven off, crack the door open, and cool for 1 hour in the oven, then remove and cool completely.

For the chestnut puree: While the Pavlova is baking, place the chestnuts into a 2-quart sauce pan with the sugar, cinnamon stick, and 1 cup of water. Bring to a boil, reduce the heat and simmer for 20 minutes, until the chestnuts are very soft. Remove from the heat, cool slightly, and puree in a food processor. Cool completely.

For the almonds: Preheat the oven to 300°F.

In a small bowl stir together the almonds, 1 teaspoon of water, sugar, cinnamon, and salt. Spread onto a baking sheet and bake for 20 minutes or until golden brown. Cool and chop.

To assemble: Whip the cream, sugar, and vanilla together until soft peaks form. Spread the chestnut puree into the center of the pavlova, leaving a 1½-inch border. Mound the whipped cream on top, drizzle on Chocolate Sauce (from page 66), and toasted almonds. Refrigerate if you aren't serving right away.

Menu

Sausage Biscuit Bites

Russian Tea

Butternut Squash Soup

Mini Open-Face
Grilled Cheese Sandwiches

Mini Chicago Sliders

Cheeses, Fruits, and Nuts

Chapter 14
Talkin' Big Book Party

We don't generally have drinks parties at the ranch because, child, if you're going to come all the way out here, we are going to feed you properly. But drinks parties have their place, and book launches are one of them. Book-writing now runs in the family with the publication of my husband's memoir, *Talkin' Big: How an Iowa Farm Boy Beat the Odds to Found and Lead One of the World's Largest Brokerage Firms*. If you haven't read it (what?!) suffice to say the title is tongue-in-cheek. Tom's had an adventurous life, full of funny stories, good laughs, and great lessons, and that's what it's about. We started celebrating in New York and then Chicago, both cities where Tom has lived and worked, before coming home to the Valley. By then it was close to Christmas and much to be jolly about.

This was an afternoon party for about sixty out in the olive orchard. We had two tables set up for food and two bars, one staffed, and one self-serve. The rule of thumb is one bartender for every fifty people, but the rule of Frances—I'm Southern, remember— is to double that, at least at the party's beginning. It is crucial to have enough bars and bartenders so people don't wait for a drink. Nothing is worse. What's more, I always have someone by the door with a tray of wine, sparkling water, and whatever. Many guests will help themselves there and bypass the bar, preventing the dreaded pile-up. I am rabid about this. As it was the late afternoon we didn't count on big drinking, but we are after all in the middle of wine country and we do like our wine. Must support the local economy.

Chilly weather and a casual festive vibe called for simple but substantial provisions. I also wanted to have Tom's favorites. The butternut squash soup and mini grilled cheese was a winning combo, warm and filling. The Chicago Sliders were yummy little steak sandwiches with a spicy tang—in homage to his beloved City—and his spicy personality. Sausage biscuits are sacred manna to a Southerner, and these mini versions Stephanie came up with were the best I've ever had. Your average pigs-in-the-blanket are poor relations by comparison, I'm telling you. An abundant cheese-fruit-nut selection and a yummy assortment of cookies and sweets rounded the table out just rightly. Overdoing it looks like trying too hard.

As a surprise, I commissioned a song for Tom by talented composer Bent Myggen, who brilliantly combined both the goofiest and most poignant parts of the story within a beautiful melody. A hastily assembled chorus comprising my fellow choir members and assorted local stars rose to the occasion and performed admirably. Tom was gob-smacked. I just tried not to cry. I failed. I am hopeless at these things.

In miraculous concurrence with the closing of the bars, guests departed and a small group of out-of-town house guests scurried inside for dinner.

At the end of a month of wall-to-wall travel, party planning, and holiday organizing, your indefatigable hostess was fatigued, I confess. With Christmas tree and mantles as decoration enough,

I kept the tables and flowers simple. Oh, and it was my birthday. The most upstaged birthday in history. Did we even sing? I can't remember. With so much else going on, my birthday was a non-event. And that's okay. I can overlook it. No really, I'm fine. Honestly, totally fine, I swear . . .

Kidding aside, sometimes your parties are about you, but mostly they are not. They are about you making your guests feel warm, welcome, and happy. Whether you are celebrating books, birthdays, graduations, grand tours, retirements, or a Tuesday, you are celebrating life and affirming that we are all in it together, so let's enjoy it.

Sausage Biscuit Bites

Makes 56

A dab of our spicy Chipotle Harissa makes this old Southern favorite California cool . . . and hot. We love Niman Ranch breakfast sausages, but any breakfast sausage link will do. Breakfast sausages tend to come in 12-ounce packs of links each, hence our count of 56 servings. The amounts are easily adapted of course, and this recipe is easily doubled or halved. These freeze beautifully and are good to have on hand for a quick hors d'oeuvre or breakfast snack.

2 (12-ounce) packages breakfast sausage links,
    or 28 links total, cooked by the package directions
1 recipe Buttermilk Biscuit Dough (page 166)
⅓ cup Chipotle Harissa (recipe below), optional

Preheat oven to 425°F. Cut the cooked sausages in half.
    Divide the dough into halves. Roll each half into a square about ¼-inch thick. Cut into 28 (2-inch) squares. Repeat with remaining half of dough. Put a dab (about ⅛ teaspoon) of the harissa in the center of each square and place a sausage half on top, on the diagonal. Pull 2 opposing corners up around the sausage and press together on top, like a pig-in-a-blanket. Arrange 1 to 2 inches apart on an ungreased or parchment-lined baking sheet, and brush lightly with the egg wash. Bake 12 to 15 minutes or until golden brown.

Chipotle Harissa

A true harissa would use seeded and rehydrated dried peppers, but we love the Southwestern smokiness (and convenience!) of the canned chipotles.

1 (7-ounce) can chipotle peppers in adobo sauce
3 tablespoons rice wine vinegar
1 clove garlic, minced
¾ teaspoon caraway seeds
½ teaspoon salt

In a blender, combine the chipotle pepper with the adobo sauce, vinegar, garlic, caraway, and salt, and blend on high speed to a smooth puree. Keep the top on the blender for a few minutes before opening to let the chili mixture settle, and open the top away from your face. The harissa will keep refrigerated for several weeks.

> **"Too many hors d'oeuvres are a sign of insecurity."**
> **—My Mother**

Russian Tea

Makes 20 servings, or about 1 gallon

Talk about a throw-back. Apart from the astonishing fact that they drink tea in Russia, I have no idea why they call it Russian Tea. Maybe someone in 1950s North Carolina thought it would scandalize her bridge club? Our version, made with natural ingredients and sans the traditional powdered drink mixes, is less sweet and absolutely delicious. The Californians, intrigued, drank it up. Easily doubled for a larger crowd. It is also good iced. And with vodka. Maybe that's why they call it Russian Tea.

1 gallon water
3 cinnamon sticks
1 heaping teaspoon whole cloves
½ a nutmeg, freshly grated
1 cup loose black tea, or 16 individual teabags, or
    equivalent
2 cups orange juice
¼ cup lemon juice
½ cup honey

Bring a gallon of water to boil and add the cinnamon sticks, cloves, and nutmeg, and then the tea. Steep for 5 to 10 minutes and drain into a metal or glass container, squeezing the tea to get every drop. While the tea is still hot, stir in the orange and lemon juices, and the honey. Add more honey or sugar if needed. Reheat, but don't boil, to serve.
    Note: Food and liquid stored in metal or glass containers tastes better than food stored in plastic. It just does.

Butternut Squash Soup

Serves 8

Spices and ginger give a lift to this favorite seasonal standby.

3 tablespoons olive oil
1 small onion, chopped
1 clove garlic, chopped
¼ teaspoon cumin
¼ teaspoon coriander
Pinch red chili flakes
1 (2-inch) slice peeled ginger root
6 cups cubed butternut squash
8 cups chicken or vegetable stock
1 teaspoon salt
¼ teaspoon pepper

Heat a Dutch oven over medium-high heat. Add the olive oil, onion, garlic, cumin, coriander, red chili, and ginger root to the pan and sauté, stirring for 3 minutes. Add the squash, stir for 1 minute more, and add the stock, salt, and pepper, and bring to a boil. Reduce the heat and simmer for 30 minutes, or until the squash is very tender. Cool to room temperature. Blend the cooled soup in batches to a smooth puree, strain if desired, and return to pot and reheat slowly.

Mini Open-Face Grilled Cheese Sandwiches

Makes 36 (2-inch) sandwiches

We like to serve these open-faced to reduce the bread-age. That said, the better the bread, the better these bites will be. Our superb local bakery, the Baker's Table in Santa Ynez, has a fantastic corn-rye bread that we use for these sandwiches. If you don't have a 2-inch round cutter, then cut into 2-inch squares.

12 slices corn rye bread
4 tablespoons salted butter, softened
1 cup grated Gruyere, Cantal, or Swiss cheese
2 teaspoons mayonnaise, preferably homemade
　(see recipe on page 42)
Pinch of cayenne pepper

Preheat the broiler.

Butter one side of each slice of bread. Using a 2-inch round cutter, cut the bread into 36 rounds and arrange on a baking tray. Combine the grated cheese, mayonnaise, and the pepper, and spread 1 heaping teaspoon of the mixture onto the unbuttered side of the bread. Heat a large sauté pan over medium-high heat and grill the pieces buttered side down until the bottoms are golden brown. Remove from the pan back to the baking tray and broil for 1 minute or until the cheese is melted and bubbly.

Note: These are also very good made with Pimento Cheese, recipe on page 42, substituting the cheese-mayonnaise mixture above.

Mini Chicago Sliders

Makes 80 (2-bite) sandwiches

This savory and spicy roast may be used to make sandwiches of any size, but we especially love it as a hearty hors d'oeuvre. Our 2-bite sandwich is made with a 10-gram Whole Wheat Brioche, which is less than half the size of a normal slider roll. If you don't want to make the rolls (we hear you), your local bakery may make a special order for you, or the small dinner rolls in grocery stores will work as well. It is best to make the roast a day or two ahead. A roast is easier to slice thinly if it has been refrigerated overnight.

4 pounds beef rump roast
2 tablespoons salt
1 tablespoon pepper
2 tablespoons Italian seasoning (see note)
½ teaspoon red chili flakes
4 tablespoons olive oil
1 onion, quartered
1 cup red wine
2–3 cups chicken stock
80 Whole Wheat Brioches or other small dinner rolls
1 cup mayonnaise
1 cup pickled vegetable giardiniera, chopped

Preheat the oven to 300°F.

Rub the roast with the salt, pepper, Italian seasoning, red pepper flakes, and oil. Heat a Dutch oven over medium high heat and sear the roast on all sides, remove roast from the pan, and add the onion and red wine. Cook and stir until the wine is reduced by half, then stir in the stock or water. In the same pot, place the meat on a rack and roast uncovered in the oven for 2 to 3 hours or to an internal temperature of 140°F. Let the roast rest before slicing, or better yet refrigerate it overnight. Save the pan with the drippings or reserve the drippings separately as you will use them later. When preparing to make the sandwiches, slice the beef as thinly as possible. Re-heat the pan drippings and warm the beef in the drippings. Split and toast the rolls, and spread with a little mayonnaise and giardiniera. Finish with the sliced beef and watch them disappear.

Note: Italian seasoning can be bought ready-made, or you can make your own by combining equal parts dried basil, marjoram, oregano, rosemary, sage, and thyme.

Whole Wheat Brioche

Makes 80 small rolls, 12 larger rolls, or 1 loaf

Allow time for the dough to rise and then to be refrigerated overnight. A digital food scale is also handy.
Note: Larger rolls or one large loaf will require longer baking times. Estimate 15 to 20 minutes for the rolls and 35 to 40 minutes for the loaf.

2 cups all-purpose flour, divided
½ cup warm water
1 tablespoon yeast
1 tablespoon sugar
1½ cups whole wheat flour
1 teaspoon salt
4 eggs, room temperature
8 tablespoons (1 stick) butter, softened

In a large bowl or the bowl of a stand mixer, whisk together ½ cup of the all-purpose flour with ½ cup warm water, yeast, and sugar and let sit for 10 minutes or until the mixture is bubbly. Add the remaining flours, salt, and eggs to the yeast mixture, slowly stirring by hand or with the dough hook until a soft dough is formed. Add a bit more water or flour as needed. Continue to knead for 5 minutes and then start to knead in the softened butter, continuing until the butter is completely incorporated, about 4 minutes more. Lightly brush the dough with olive oil or butter and cover with a towel or plastic wrap and allow to rise at room temperature until doubled in volume, about 1 hour. Punch down the dough and fold in on itself, cover, and refrigerate overnight.

Remove the dough from the refrigerator. Pinch dough into 10-gram portions, about the size of a quarter in diameter, for 2-bite sandwiches, or into the size you desire. Use the palms of your hands to roll the dough into small balls. Instead of flour, use drops of water to moisten the rolling surface to help "grab" the dough. Place the rolls on a parchment-lined tray about 2 inches apart, cover with a towel, and allow to rise for 50 minutes. Preheat the oven to 350°F. When risen, bake the rolls for 12 to 15 minutes or until golden brown. Cool on a rack and store in an airtight container until ready to use. Freeze for up to 3 months.

Cheeses, Fruits, and Nuts

To create a gorgeous cheese plate for a crowd, think about texture, flavor, and fullness. Offer no more than four so it doesn't get fussy, and include one from each category:

Soft: Reblochon, Camembert, or a triple-cream like
    Explorateur
Firm: Cantal, Parmesan, Pecorino, Manchego
Blue: Roquefort, Stilton, Gorgonzola
Aged: Asiago, Cheddar, Gouda, Gruyère

It's also nice to have a mix of goat's, cow's, or sheep's cheeses. If one of them is particularly pungent, separate it from the others so it doesn't overwhelm. Have sliced baguettes and a variety of crackers, and a selection of one or two dried fruits, such as apricots, cherries, or figs. Fresh apple and pear slices are good, as are raw or roasted almonds, walnuts, pistachios, or pecans.

Pots of honey, chutney, or preserves are often done, but they do get messy and we don't love sweet with savory. Up to you. The important thing is to have a platter or tray that is nice and full-looking. Gauge quantities depending on what other food you have. And lastly, be sure to buy what you like, so you will enjoy the leftovers. Cheese does freeze well and can always be used in salads or other cooking.

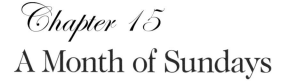

Chapter 15
A Month of Sundays

Sunday night suppers at Rancho La Zaca have become a ritual in themselves, a lovely way to end one week and begin a new one. We almost always have company, almost always including St. Mark's rector the Reverend Randall Day and his husband and tenor extraordinaire Bill Hurbaugh, hence my prevailing upon them to write the foreword for this book. The suppers, Randall, Bill, and whomever else comes along, are a regular thing we look forward to like seeing a favorite painting. Every stroke is familiar, and yet there is always something new. Sometimes I make a fuss over the table, most times I don't. Our Sunday night menus are the same way. Most times they are our simple, comfort food favorites, a pot of pasta or stew, in a quantity ample to accommodate the last-minute invitees that I am infamous for. That Stephanie has not come after me with a rolling pin is a wonder, bless her. Here are menus for a month of Sunday suppers, and even more good news: They work for weekdays, too.

Menu 1

New Potatoes
with Mushrooms and Arugula

Pan Seared Salmon
with Lemon Caper
Olive Vinaigrette

Bread and Butter Pudding

Menu 2

Chicken Country Captain

Broccoli Salad

Buttermilk Biscuits

Persimmon Pudding

Menu 3

Blue Cheese Pecans

Warm Escarole Salad
with Pancetta and Egg

*Mushroom and Asparagus
Busiati*

*Ricotta Almond
Chess Pie*

Menu 4

*Frisee, Fennel, and Green
Bean Salad*

Lamb and White Bean Stew
with Pistou

Poached Pears
with Crème Fraîche

New Potatoes
with Mushrooms and Arugula
Serves 4

Choose the smallest new potatoes you can find. If they are too big to be bite-sized, cut them in half or quarters.

1½ pounds new potatoes
1 small head of garlic, cloves separated but not peeled
⅓ cup olive oil, divided
Kosher salt
½ pound mushrooms such as shiitake, chanterelle, portobello, oyster, or combination
1 teaspoon grainy mustard
1 tablespoon red or white wine vinegar
2 cups arugula leaves or mixed greens
Freshly ground pepper

Preheat oven to 300°F.

In a roasting pan, toss potatoes and garlic with 2 tablespoons of the oil and 2 teaspoons kosher salt. Bake 1 to 1½ hours, or until tender. Reduce the heat if they are cooking too fast and stir them occasionally to prevent sticking.

While the potatoes cook, sauté the mushrooms in a 12-inch sauté pan over high heat with a tablespoon of the oil. Cook just until they begin to brown and release their juices. Set aside.

Whisk together the mustard and vinegar, continue whisking in the remaining olive oil in a thin stream so the dressing emulsifies.

Remove the potatoes from the oven and set aside the garlic. Toss the potatoes and mushrooms together with the dressing. Before serving, toss with the arugula. Season with pepper and more salt if needed. You will have none of this leftover.

Note: Bring the roasted garlic to the table in a separate little bowl. It is wonderful squeezed onto bread or toast.

Pan Seared Salmon
with Lemon-Caper-Olive Vinaigrette
Serves 4

Salmon
4 (6-ounce) salmon filets, prepared as on page 112

Lemon-Caper-Olive Vinaigrette
No cooking required for this splendid, all-purpose Lemon-Caper-Olive sauce for fish, chicken, or vegetables. It is ready in the time it takes to chop the ingredients. Can be made ahead and refrigerated for several days. Let it come to room temperature, or warm it gently, before serving. Use best-quality, flavorful olives, such as Kalamata, Lucques, or Castelvetrano.

4 tablespoons sliced olives
2 tablespoons finely chopped red onion
2 tablespoons chopped capers
2 tablespoons chopped fresh basil
1 teaspoon chopped fresh thyme or oregano
1 tablespoon lemon juice
2 tablespoons red wine vinegar
6 tablespoons olive oil
Salt and pepper to taste

Whisk together all ingredients, and season further to taste.

Opposite: If you don't have the correct size tablecloth, improvise, as I did here. A cloth smaller than your table may be treated as a sort of runner or coverlet. A too-big cloth can often be folded, draped, or "hemmed" with duct tape (yes!) at the last minute.

Bread and Butter Pudding

Serves 6

Our famous Valley neighbor, writer and crooner Shaun Cassidy said this was the best dessert he ever had. We like the recipe's simplicity and ease of scaling down for 2 or 4. It is also a good use for less-than-fresh bread.

1 French baguette, cut into ¼-inch slices
8 ounces unsalted butter, at room temperature,
    plus 3 tablespoons for buttering the ramekins
½ cup chopped bittersweet chocolate
1¼ cups whole milk
1 cup half-and-half
3 whole eggs
3 egg yolks
4½ tablespoons sugar, plus 4 tablespoons for
    the ramekins
1 teaspoon vanilla
¼ teaspoon salt
1 tablespoon turbinado sugar, optional
Whipped Cream (page 148) or Vanilla Ice Cream
    (page 23) for serving, if desired

Butter six 8-ounce ramekins and sprinkle each ramekin lightly with about 2 teaspoons of sugar.

Lightly butter both sides of each baguette slice. Place a single layer of buttered baguette onto the bottom of the ramekins, cutting and trimming as necessary to fit. Sprinkle half of the chocolate over the bread. Add another layer of baguette slices and chopped chocolate, and end with a layer of baguette slices. Whisk together the milk, half-and-half, whole eggs, yolks, sugar, vanilla, and salt. Strain and pour evenly among the ramekins, just covering the bread. Sprinkle with the turbinado sugar if using, and let sit for 30 minutes. Preheat the oven to 350°F.

Bake the puddings for 30 to 40 minutes, until lightly browned.

Serve warm with whipped cream or vanilla ice cream.

Chicken Country Captain

Serves 6

An updated version of the old Lowcountry recipe originating when the ship captains began to bring back curry and spices from the East. Any combination of white and dark meat chicken is okay. Our version is fork-friendly with its bite-size pieces of boneless chicken. You may also add spicy bulk sausage, crumbled and browned separately, and added to the mix when the chicken is added before its final simmer.

1½–2 pounds boneless chicken, cut into 1-inch pieces
Salt and pepper
4 tablespoons unsalted butter, divided
1 medium onion, chopped
1 celery stalk, chopped
½ red bell pepper, seeded and chopped
1 tablespoon chopped garlic
1 teaspoon minced fresh ginger
1 teaspoon chopped fresh thyme
2 teaspoons yellow curry powder
½ teaspoon ground cumin
¼ cup flour
1¼ cups peeled, seeded, and chopped tomatoes,
    or 1 (15-ounce) can whole tomatoes, crushed,
    undrained
2 cups chicken stock, hot
6 tablespoons white wine
2 tablespoons lemon juice
½ cup chopped golden raisins, optional
½ cup chopped toasted almonds
¼ cup parsley

Season the chicken with salt and pepper.

In a 1-gallon pot over medium-high heat, add 1 tablespoon of butter. In batches, sear the chicken on all sides until golden brown. Remove from the pot and set aside.

Add the remaining butter to the pan. Stir in the onion and cook for 3 minutes. Add the celery and peppers and cook 3 minutes more. Add the garlic, ginger, thyme, curry powder, and cumin, and cook for 5 more minutes. Stir in the flour and cook for 2 minutes more. Add the tomatoes, and then slowly whisk in the hot chicken stock, stirring constantly to avoid lumps.

Add the wine, lemon juice, and chopped raisins if using, and bring to a boil. Lower the heat and simmer for 10 minutes

Add the chicken, cover, and simmer 10 minutes more. Serve over rice and garnish with toasted almonds, chopped parsley, and more raisins if desired.

Broccoli Salad

Makes 6 servings

Adapted from my friend and fellow Southerner Alex Hitz's Broccoli Slaw in his wonderful book My Beverly Hills Kitchen. *It is best made several hours or even the day before.*

1 head broccoli, cut into florets
2 cups diced green cabbage
2 cups thinly sliced red cabbage
1 yellow bell pepper, diced
1 shallot, minced
½ cup chopped fresh dill
1 teaspoon salt
½ teaspoon pepper
Dressing (recipe below)

Bring a large pot of salted water to a boil. Blanch the broccoli for 30 seconds, turn into a colander, and rinse under cold running water. Pat dry. Put the broccoli in a large mixing bowl with the cabbages, yellow pepper, shallot, and dill. Toss in the dressing and refrigerate for 3 hours or overnight. Stir and season with salt and pepper again before serving.

To make the dressing
In a small bowl whisk together:
   ¼ cup mayonnaise
   ¼ cup sour cream
   1 tablespoon Dijon mustard
   1 teaspoon lemon juice
   Salt and pepper to taste

Buttermilk Biscuits

Makes 24

The addition of 2 to 3 tablespoons of chopped herbs such as rosemary or dill, or a cup of grated sharp cheddar cheese and/or chopped, thick-cut bacon, make delicious variations.

Note: For better biscuits, you want to work the dough as little as possible, so if you are using a biscuit cutter, press straight down and don't twist. Same if you are using a knife; don't saw, just cut straight down, quickly and with confidence. For maximum rise, flip the biscuit over before placing on the baking sheet to counteract the downward pointing biscuit edges. Gather and roll the scraps just once. After that the dough gets tough.

2 cups all-purpose flour
2 cups whole wheat pastry flour
2 tablespoons baking powder
½ teaspoon baking soda
1 tablespoon sugar
1 teaspoon cream of tartar
1 teaspoon salt
1 cup cold butter, cut into small cubes
1½ cups buttermilk
1 egg, well beaten

Preheat the oven to 425°F.

In a large bowl whisk together the flours, baking powder, baking soda, sugar, cream of tartar, and salt. If you are adding herbs, cheese, and/or bacon, add them here. Add the butter cubes and cut together with a pastry blender, 2 knives, or your fingers, until the mixture resembles coarse crumbs and the butter bits are pea-sized. Make a well in the center and add the buttermilk all at once. Stir together with a spoon in a few quick strokes, just until the mixture binds together. Turn out onto a floured surface and knead for 8 to 10 strokes, dusting with flour as needed, just until the dough comes together. Overdoing it makes the dough tough.

Roll or pat the dough to ¾-inch thick. Use a biscuit cutter or drinking glass turned upside down to cut into rounds, or use a knife to cut into 2-inch squares. Brush the biscuits lightly with the egg wash and arrange on an ungreased or parchment-lined baking sheet. Bake for 12 to 15 minutes until golden brown.

It never gets old: the view from our porch. As for the table, with a bunch of clear glass containers—any and everything from wine bottles to jelly jars—you can make the most beautiful centerpieces. They can be as simple (like this one) or as elaborate (like Chapter 11) as you like. Add a bevy of candles, and boom, you're a genius.

Persimmon Pudding

Serves 6

For this recipe we use the Asian Hachiya persimmon, which is long, acorn–shaped, and should only be used when fully ripe. Hachiya persimmons are sold at groceries and farmers' market in the fall. They are most often sold unripe and may take up to a week to ripen, so plan accordingly. You could also use the native American Persimmon Diaspyros Virginiana, which grows in the Southeast as well as California. But of course everything grows in California. This is a favorite fall dessert at Rancho la Zaca.

Note: The persimmon pulp freezes beautifully.

2 cups puréed persimmon pulp
1 cup light brown sugar or coconut sugar, loosely packed
3 eggs
6 tablespoons melted butter, plus more for the pan
1½ cups all-purpose flour
1 teaspoon baking soda
1 teaspoon cinnamon
½ teaspoon salt
1 cup buttermilk

Preheat the oven to 325°F.

Butter a 3-quart Pyrex dish or 6 (1-cup) ramekins.

In a 2-quart bowl whisk together the persimmon puree, sugar, eggs, and melted butter. In another bowl whisk together the flour, baking soda, cinnamon, and salt.

Fold the flour mixture into the persimmon mixture alternately with the buttermilk in 3 batches, beginning and ending with flour.

Pour into the buttered baking dish or dishes and bake for 45 minutes to 1 hour, until a toothpick inserted in the center comes out clean. Serve the pudding warm with whipped cream or hot cream.

Blue Cheese Pecans

Makes 2 cups

2 ounces blue cheese, softened
2 tablespoons unsalted butter, softened
2 tablespoons sugar
4 tablespoons all-purpose flour
½ teaspoon salt
2 cups pecan halves

Preheat the oven to 300°F.

With a fork and your fingertips, blend together the blue cheese, butter, sugar, flour, and salt. Add the pecans and massage the cheese and butter mixture into the nuts. Spread the nuts on an ungreased, parchment-lined baking sheet and bake for 15 to 20 minutes or until the crust on the nuts is starting to brown. Remove from the oven and cool completely before serving. Store in an airtight container for up to a week, or freeze.

Warm Escarole Salad
with Pancetta and Egg
Serves 6

This is a delicious salad and impressive served family style. Bacon may be substituted for the pancetta. The smoked paprika adds a distinct special flavor but may be substituted with regular paprika. Have all your ingredients measured and ready to go, as the preparation moves quickly once begun.

3 tablespoons olive oil
Juice from ½ lemon
½ teaspoon smoked paprika
½ teaspoon salt
¼ teaspoon pepper
1 cup plus 2 tablespoons flat-leaf parsley leaves
4 tablespoons chopped pancetta
3 eggs
1 clove garlic, minced
1 shallot, chopped
3 heads escarole, green parts removed and cut into
     1-inch squares
¼ cup chives, chopped in 1-inch pieces
¼ cup shaved asiago cheese

Make the dressing by whisking together the olive oil, lemon juice, paprika, salt and pepper, and 2 tablespoons of the parsley, and set aside. In a 12-inch sauté pan over medium heat, cook the chopped pancetta or bacon until brown and crisp. While the bacon is cooking, begin frying the eggs in a separate pan. Remove bacon and set aside to drain, leaving the fat in the pan.

When the eggs are done, set aside or keep them warm in a 250°F oven. Stir the garlic and shallot into the pan with the pancetta fat, then turn up the heat and add the escarole, stirring for 30 seconds, until just starting to wilt. Remove from the heat and add the remaining parsley, chives, salt, and pepper. Toss with ⅔ of the dressing and arrange the salad on a platter. Top with the fried eggs and shaved asiago, and drizzle with the remaining dressing.

Mushroom and Asparagus Busiati

Serves 6

Earthy, soothing, and flavorful, this mushroom and asparagus pasta may be made with any variety pasta, though we favor the long, rolled busiati which magically clings to every drop of sauce and flavor. Pappardelle is also good with this dish. Either the asparagus or the mushrooms may be omitted, but compensate by increasing the other. Like many pasta dishes, this one is best cooked al minuto.

Note: If you are following our menu and serving the Warm Escarole Salad, you might want to forgo the pancetta again in the pasta. Then again, you might not.

4 tablespoons olive oil, divided

3 tablespoons chopped pancetta

4 tablespoons butter, divided

1½ pounds wild mushrooms, any variety or mixture

1 shallot, minced

1 clove garlic, minced

1 pound asparagus, cut into 1-inch pieces

2–4 tablespoons lemon juice

2 tablespoons chopped herbs, such as thyme, oregano, or rosemary

½ cup cream, optional

¼ cup chopped parsley

1 teaspoon salt

½ teaspoon pepper

1 pound busiati (or any) pasta

¾ cup grated Parmesan, plus more for serving

Set a gallon-size pot of salted water on the stove to boil, so you can cook the pasta while you are making the sauce.

Meanwhile in another large pot over medium heat, add 1 tablespoon of oil and the pancetta. Cook and stir for 3 to 5 minutes until the pancetta is crisp. Remove the pancetta with a slotted spoon and set aside. Increase the heat to medium-high. Add 1 more tablespoon of oil and 2 tablespoons butter, and add the mushrooms. Cook and stir for 5 minutes. Now begin cooking the pasta according to package directions. Now back to the mushrooms: Add the shallot, garlic, and asparagus, and cook for 3 minutes more. Add the lemon juice and herbs and season with salt and pepper. Add the pancetta back to the pan with the cream and parsley. When the pasta is ready, reserve ½ cup of the cooking water before draining. Toss the cooked pasta with the sauce, add the Parmesan cheese, and moisten with the reserved pasta water or more olive oil or butter if needed. Adjust the seasoning and serve with more Parmesan on the side.

Getting Fresh

We are lucky to have some of the best farmers in California throughout our Central Coast region, growing everything from avocados, lettuces, tomatoes, and herbs, to nuts, dates, mulberries, elderberries, and more. All are sold at year-round farmers' markets in our area, so we almost never have to worry about finding fresh ingredients. Be sure you use the freshest ingredients you can find, and if you can't find them, make something else.

Ricotta Almond Chess Pie

Makes 1 (9-inch) pie

Chess pie is one of those inscrutable Southern delicacies whose simple ingredients—butter, flour, sugar, and eggs—belie its power to please. Its origins and etymology are debated, but my favorite story is that when someone asked the cook what she was making, she said in her country dialect, "Oh, 'jes pie."

This is also, obviously, a cheesecake as it is made with Ricotta cheese. But when I tasted it and double-checked the ingredients, yep, it tasted like 'jes pie, but with the wave of Stephanie's magic flavor wand. Use the best quality ricotta you can find. If you don't have superfine or caster sugar, whiz regular granulated sugar in the blender. The almond flour gives a delicious nutty flavor and has no gluten.

1¼ cups superfine or caster sugar, plus 2 tablespoons

2 cups almond flour, plus 2 tablespoons

Salt

½ cup butter, plus extra for the pan

Finely grated zest of 1 lemon

1 tablespoon lemon juice

1 teaspoon vanilla extract

1 teaspoon almond extract

4 eggs, separated into yolks and whites

15 ounces ricotta cheese (1¾ cups), room temperature

⅓ cup sliced almonds

Powdered sugar for dusting

Combine 2 tablespoons of the sugar and 2 tablespoons of the almond flour in a small bowl with a pinch of salt. Butter a 10-inch springform pan, and coat the pan with the almond/sugar mixture, tapping out the excess.

Preheat the oven to 350°F.

Cream the butter and remaining sugar together in the bowl of an electric mixer until light and fluffy, about 5 minutes. Add the lemon zest, juice, vanilla, and almond extracts, and 1 teaspoon salt, and cream 1 minute more. Add the egg yolks one at a time, beating after each addition, and beat 3 minutes more after the last addition. Add the remaining almond flour, mixing until just blended, about 20 seconds, then add the ricotta and blend for 10 seconds more. In a large clean bowl, beat the egg whites until stiff but not dry. Fold in ¼ of the beaten whites into the ricotta mixture to lighten, then fold in the remaining whites.

Spread into the prepared pan, sprinkle with the almonds, and bake for 60 to 70 minutes or until a pick inserted in the middle comes out clean. Allow to cool at room temperature and then refrigerate. Dust liberally with powdered sugar to serve.

Frisée, Fennel, and Green Bean Salad

Serves 4

Simple, unusual, and delicious.

2 heads frisée lettuce
½ pound green beans, trimmed
1 large fennel bulb
¼ cup parsley leaves
¼ cup chopped dill
2 tablespoons sliced red onion
1½ tablespoons lemon juice
3 tablespoons olive oil
2 teaspoons whole grain mustard
Salt and pepper

Trim the frisée, leaving only the tender white and yellow leaves, wash, and dry in a salad spinner.

Put a small pot of salted water on to boil. Add the trimmed green beans and blanch for 1 minute. Rinse under cool water and drain well on paper towels.

Trim the bottom and the top of the fennel, trim the tough outer leaves, and thinly slice the bulb on a mandolin. Combine the fennel with the frisée, green beans, parsley, and dill. In a small bowl stir together the lemon juice, olive oil, mustard, salt, and pepper, and toss with the vegetables. Adjust seasonings before serving.

Lamb and White Bean Stew
with Pistou

Serves 6 to 8

This is adapted from my now seemingly ancient Atlanta at Table *and is a longtime favorite go-to for casual, easy, do-ahead dinners. While the stew is simmering, make the pistou. Serve with toasted buttery baguettes or a crusty French or sourdough bread.*

Lamb Stew
2 pounds lamb shoulder, cut into ¾-inch pieces
2 teaspoons salt
1 teaspoon pepper
3 tablespoons olive oil
2 cups chopped onions
1½ cups chopped carrots
1 cup chopped celery
1–2 cloves garlic, minced
1 (15-ounce) can whole tomatoes, with juices, or 2 cups
     peeled, seeded, and chopped fresh tomatoes
2 cups chopped green cabbage
½ cup dried porcini, soaked in 1 cup of boiling water for
     30 minutes or longer
1 tablespoon chopped fresh marjoram
1 teaspoon chopped fresh thyme
6 cups chicken, beef, or lamb stock
2 (15-ounce) cans Great Northern white beans, or the
     equivalent of home cooked, rinsed and drained

Pistou
4–5 cloves garlic, minced
1 teaspoon coarse sea salt
¾ cup grated Fontina or Gouda cheese
¼ cup grated parmesan cheese
2 tablespoons olive oil

For the lamb stew: Heat a large, 2-gallon pot over high heat. Season the lamb with half of the salt and pepper. Add the oil to the hot pot and sear the lamb in batches, removing from the pot and setting aside.

(Continued on page 176)

Add the onion, carrot, celery, and garlic to the pot and cook over moderate heat until soft, about 5 minutes. Add the tomatoes and their juices, breaking them up with a spoon. Add the cabbage, the mushrooms with their liquid, and the herbs. Increase the heat to high and stir up any brown bits from the bottom of the pot. Add the stock and reserved lamb with juices back to the pan and bring to a simmer. Cover, reduce the heat to low, and simmer for 1 hour, stirring occasionally. Add the beans and continue cooking for another 30 minutes, or until the lamb is fork tender.

Meanwhile, make the pistou.

For the pistou: Mash the garlic, sea salt, cheeses, and olive oil together in a mortar and pestle, or whir together in a food processor. Stir in ½ cup of the lamb stew broth and set aside.

Stir the pistou into the lamb stew just before serving.

To make your own crème fraîche, stir 2 tablespoons of cultured sour cream into 1 cup of cream. Cover, leaving a small air hole, and let sit at room temperature for 2 to 3 days, until thickened. Will keep for several days refrigerated.

Poached Pears
with Crème Fraîche
Serves 4

You can use any variety of spice that you like, and a section of a scraped vanilla bean is fantastic. Red wine makes a nice alternative to the white.

4 small ripe pears, any variety
3 cups white wine
1 cup sugar or honey
1 cinnamon stick
6 cracked peppercorns
1 star anise
8 ounces crème fraîche

Peel the pears, leaving them whole with the stem intact or coring and slicing them into sixths.

Bring the wine, sugar, cinnamon, peppercorns, and anise to a boil in a pot that fits the pears in a single layer. Add the pears to the pot and simmer for 25 minutes to poach the whole pear and 10 minutes to poach the wedges. Remove from the heat and allow the pears to cool for an hour in the liquid. Remove the pears and return the pot to the fire and simmer until the poaching liquid is reduced by half. Strain out the spices and reserve the liquid.

Whip the crème fraîche until light peaks form.

Spoon a big dollop of crème fraîche onto each plate along with 1 pear and drizzle the reserved poaching liquid over all.

Variation: Serve the poached pears with chocolate sauce and ice cream and you have "Poire Belle Hélène," created in 1864 by legendary French chef Auguste Escoffier and named after the operetta La Belle Hélène by Jacques Offenbach.

Acknowledgments

My dearest darlingest husband Tom is the funnest and most generous host I know, and this book would not have happened without him. Thank you, my love.

It also wouldn't have happened without Stephanie Valentine, whose creativity, skill, and grace in the kitchen happily spill into every aspect of her life and into the lives of those around her. What a gift she is to all of us. I have never known a better cook than she, nor a better person.

Ranch Manager Wyatt Cromer is a wonder, and I wonder how we got so lucky to find him. Thank you, Wyatt. I will say the same for my assistant Stephanie Chin: Thank you dear, fabulous, ridiculously efficient and lovely lady. And thank you dear Perfect Boto, for your faith, your loyalty and your smile.

Janice Shay not only designed this book but helped conceive it. Her encouragement every step of the way walked me back from the precipice more than once. She is a treasure and a treasured friend.

To my wonderful agent Beth Davey of Davey Literary Media, thank you for always being there and for being so dang smart. Thank you to Skyhorse Editor Leah Zarra and the Skyhorse Publishing team for taking me on yet again.

Thanks again to the Rancho La Zaca team to whom this book is dedicated, who work so earnestly and cheerfully among and behind the scenes: Felipe Hernandez, Patricia Lopez, Jackie Elliott, Isaac "Maestro" Bonilla, and Juan Garcia.

Speaking of earnest and cheerful, Mary "Dede" Wood, Renee Kelleher, and Molly Ballantine stepped into the breach, saved the day, and rocked the photo shoots. Bless your sweet, stylish, talented hearts, and boy am I grateful for you. Floral and event designer (and Dede's daughter) Mindy Rice's superlative work graces several chapters of this book and never ceases to amaze and inspire. Mindy is the bomb. And speaking of flowers, Jenna Vath and Scott Young of Florabundance, you are the best.

Photographs make all the difference in books like this, and the photographs here make it sing. Thanks and praise to Aaron Delesie, Tiffany Evitts, John Fitzpatrick, Tria Giovan, Christy Gutzeit, Deborah Whitlaw Llewellyn (glorious food!), and Lauren Porcher. The not-so-great photographs that look like they were taken on an iPhone by a) someone in a hurry, or b) someone on her fourth glass of wine, are by me.

To Randall Day and William Hurbaugh, thank you for all the Sundays past and future, for your beautiful Foreword (I will try to live up to it), and for everything you do and are.

And finally, for your inspiration, hospitality, flowers, friendship, and for your beautiful examples as hosts, thank you Dani Hahn, Alex Hitz, Nina Griscom, Roya and Bahman Irvani, James Landon, Charlotte Moss, Carolyne Roehm, Margot Shaw, Martha Stewart, Louise Strauss, Caroline Trask, and to the memories of Ryan Gainey, Rena Harris, and my mama, Ruth Clark, whose advice and presence in entertaining and all things I still miss every day. Sister Duvall Fuqua and other sister Hollye Jacobs, I love you. Thank you for helping me get here in one piece.

My friend Anne Louise Evans told me years ago that the composer J. S. Bach began each composition with the letters JJ, for *Jesu Juva*, Jesus help me; and ended with SDG, *Soli Deo Gloria*, to God Alone Glory. I have written those prayers into my own work ever since, and into my life. Thank you, Annie Lou, and thank you God.

SDG,
Frances

Conversion Charts

METRIC AND IMPERIAL CONVERSIONS
(These conversions are rounded for convenience)

Ingredient	Cups/Tablespoons/Teaspoons	Ounces	Grams/Milliliters
Butter	1 cup/16 tablespoons/2 sticks	8 ounces	230 grams
Cheese, shredded	1 cup	4 ounces	110 grams
Cream cheese	1 tablespoon	0.5 ounce	14.5 grams
Cornstarch	1 tablespoon	0.3 ounce	8 grams
Flour, all-purpose	1 cup/1 tablespoon	4.5 ounces/0.3 ounce	125 grams/8 grams
Flour, whole wheat	1 cup	4 ounces	120 grams
Fruit, dried	1 cup	4 ounces	120 grams
Fruits or veggies, chopped	1 cup	5 to 7 ounces	145 to 200 grams
Fruits or veggies, pureed	1 cup	8.5 ounces	245 grams
Honey, maple syrup, or corn syrup	1 tablespoon	0.75 ounce	20 grams
Liquids: cream, milk, water, or juice	1 cup	8 fluid ounces	240 milliliters
Oats	1 cup	5.5 ounces	150 grams
Salt	1 teaspoon	0.2 ounce	6 grams
Spices: cinnamon, cloves, ginger, or nutmeg (ground)	1 teaspoon	0.2 ounce	5 milliliters
Sugar, brown, firmly packed	1 cup	7 ounces	200 grams
Sugar, white	1 cup/1 tablespoon	7 ounces/0.5 ounce	200 grams/12.5 grams
Vanilla extract	1 teaspoon	0.2 ounce	4 grams

OVEN TEMPERATURES

Fahrenheit	Celsius	Gas Mark
225°	110°	1/4
250°	120°	1/2
275°	140°	1
300°	150°	2
325°	160°	3
350°	180°	4
375°	190°	5
400°	200°	6
425°	220°	7
450°	230°	8

Index